WHOLESALE SOURCING

A Step-by-Step Guide for eCommerce Businesses

Charlene Anderson and Darla Flack

Wholesale Sourcing Experts

JACKSON, WYOMING

Printed in the United States of America

Copy Editing by Georgene Harkness

First Printing, 2014

ISBN 978-1503384125

Wholesale Sourcing Experts
PO Box 10550
Jackson, WY 83002

www.WholesaleSourcingExperts.com

CONTENTS

An Introduction to Wholesale Sourcing 7

The Wholesale Players 13

Setting Yourself Up For Success 19

Finding Wholesalers 31

Working With Wholesalers 37

Trade Shows, Markets and Marts.............43

Closing the Deal 59

Working with Sales Reps 85

Bringing Products to Market....................89

Managing the Details..................................97

Evaluating Products 101

Outsourcing the Work...............................105

Glossary 115

Business Registration 127

Sales Tax Registration..............................135

Tools, Supplies and Suppliers We Use....................143

Limits of Liability and Disclaimer of Warranty.....147

INTRODUCTION

Wholesale sourcing is one of the most misunderstood and feared aspects of owning an eCommerce business. To many people, it seems exotic and unattainable, but it isn't. Brick and mortar shop owners have been buying wholesale since Wilma Flintstone shopped at Safestone's. All it takes is some preparation, research, and a willingness to do the work when others are ready to give up.

We have over 40 years of wholesale buying experience, purchasing for both brick and mortar stores and eCommerce businesses. We've been to over 100 trade shows, have dealt with sales reps and brokers, and have purchased inventory from every continent except Antarctica. We've learned a lot along the way, and we are now going to share it with you.

You are going to learn what you need to have in place before you start contacting wholesalers, how to find and contact them, and how to grow your business once you are onboard the wholesale train. We will also help you navigate trade shows, negotiate with suppliers, and, should things go wrong, how to deal with those issues.

We look at this book as a college course in wholesale sourcing. And because of that, you'll have homework at the end of each chapter. Successfully completing these homework assignments will help set you up for success, so don't ignore it. It's time to stop dreaming and start doing ... so let's get started!

AN INTRODUCTION TO WHOLESALE SOURCING

Wholesale sourcing is a hot topic in the eCommerce world. It seems that every group and every coach is promoting wholesale sourcing as the next big thing. Well, we're here to tell you, it's not. It's not the next big thing, it is **the** big thing, and has been since the dawn of time.

Wholesale sourcing gives you opportunities to grow your business in ways that no other sourcing method can provide. Thrift store products can provide huge margins, liquidation sources can provide products in quantity, and arbitrage allows you to leverage markets. But only wholesale provides you with consistent, repeatable products that you can sell year after year.

You don't need to be near a big city with lots of stores to source wholesale. We live in two very isolated, rural areas ... Charlene's closest Target is over 120 miles away and Darla's is 100 miles away. We are living proof that wholesale sourcing can be done from anywhere.

So exactly what is wholesale sourcing? In a nutshell, wholesale sourcing is buying goods from a manufacturer, distributor, or broker, with the intention of reselling the items. That's a pretty simple definition for a complex process. To put it in perspective, think about brick and mortar stores in your local town ... the bookstore, the gourmet food store, or the hobby shop. Where do they get their inventory? From wholesalers! They find sources for the products they want to carry in their stores, contact them, and purchase the products.

Wholesale sourcing for an eCommerce business works the same way. You find products and then sell the products. But there are a lot of details between those two steps that you will have to master, and there are subtle differences between sourcing for a brick and mortar store and an eCommerce business. You'll find out more about those differences in upcoming chapters, and how you can capitalize on them.

So how did we learn about wholesale? We've been at it for a long time, and have seen it from both sides of the table. Born into an entrepreneurial family, Charlene's parents owned a manufacturing company, so she began her business education from the wholesaler's point of view. Charlene opened a brick and mortar yarn store in Hawaii in 1984, at a time when the Internet was in its infancy and business was still done face-to-face or over the phone. She would order from a catalog, either mailing in an order or calling it in over the phone. If she was lucky, a sales rep would call and show her new products and take her order. Things took longer to get done. The speed that products came to market was slower.

With the growth of the Internet, business began to change. We started buying and selling products through local computer bulletin boards. Companies began taking orders through e-mail. Slowly, businesses began to grasp the power of the Internet. Our suppliers began to put up rudimentary web sites so we could see their new products. Things were getting easier and moving faster.

And then came two game changers: Amazon in 1994 and eBay in 1995. The launch of these two companies changed the way the world does business. Geographic limitations ceased to exist. You could start a business with a few dollars. You didn't have to have a brick and mortar store, you didn't have to hire employees, and you could fit the hours you worked on your business around other things in your life.

Charlene closed her brick and mortar store in 1997 and began selling the same product lines on eBay. In 2002, when Amazon opened Marketplace for third-party sellers, she started selling there. When Amazon introduced the Fulfillment by Amazon program in 2008, the world shifted on its axis. No longer limited by storage space, Charlene moved more and more of her products to Amazon, having them handle storage and fulfillment through the FBA program. It has allowed her to grow her business to one that does mid-six figure annual sales, on part-time hours and without employees or warehouse space.

Darla has also been part of an entrepreneurial family from birth. Her father owned a jewelry and clock/watch repair brick and mortar store until he passed away. Wholesale sourcing was a big part of that business. After attending college she worked for one of the Big Six public accounting firms in the world, and then she moved on to owning her own business as an accountant for five businesses, all of whom had relationships with wholesalers. These businesses ranged from a flower store to a well service, so Darla has worked at the extremes of the marketplace.

Darla started selling on eBay in 2007. She sold products from her involvement with a multi-level marketing company and turned that into owning her own liquidation service that continues to this day. In 2012, Darla moved most of her business to Amazon. Wholesale accounts are an integral part of her business model, and based on her knowledge and experience Darla actively sought out relationships with sales reps to make her business even more lucrative.

So what does all this have to do with learning wholesale sourcing? A lot. We source wholesale for our business, and we've been doing it a long time. Charlene's sourcing is 99% wholesale, and Darla's is 70%. We've been sourcing wholesale for as long as we can remember. We have developed processes and procedures that allow us to find good products and sell them for a profit. And we are going to tell you how we do it.

What we won't do is provide you with lists of products to buy, and we won't tell you our sources. What we will do is tell you how to find, research, and complete purchases from wholesalers so you can successfully grow your business. You'll learn what we did right, and what we did wrong. While we wholeheartedly agree on the basics of wholesale sourcing, we do some things differently. You'll find out why we do things the way we do. We won't keep secrets and we won't leave things out.

We can't help you make the decision as to exactly what to sell. What we can do is show you how to find wholesalers, navigate trade shows, and help you feel confident and comfortable throughout the entire process of wholesale sourcing.

It might sound dramatic to say wholesale sourcing will change your life, but trust us; it will. If you've ever spent an entire evening removing Tuesday Morning clearance stickers, you'll see. Now let's get started.

CHAPTER 1 HOMEWORK

- Identify three reasons why you want to begin sourcing from wholesalers

THE WHOLESALE PLAYERS

Wholesale sourcing brings a whole group of new players into the game. Here is a brief rundown on who is who in the wholesale game.

MANUFACTURERS

Manufacturers make products. They are the first level of product sourcing. Buying from a manufacturer is often the least expensive way to purchase products.

Plus:

- They know their products.
- They have the cheapest prices.

Minus:

- Product line may be limited.
- If minimum orders can't be spread across many products the numbers may not work.
- Hot deals may not always be presented … these are often saved for distributors.

- You aren't always notified of product changes.

DISTRIBUTOR

This term is often used interchangeably with the term "wholesaler." A distributor may supply products from just one manufacturer, or can supply products from several different manufacturers. Distributors have inventory in stock in their warehouses.

Plus:

- Many product lines
- May have sales reps
- May offer special deals, such as free shipping or a percentage off

Minus:

- Price may be higher

BROKER

A broker is a company who sells or arranges transactions for the account of others in exchange for a commission. A broker does not carry inventory in a warehouse ... they are a middleman and pass on orders to distributors or manufacturers.

SALES REPS

A sales rep is a person or organization designated by a company to solicit business on its behalf, usually in a specified territory. Sales reps are so important to your business that we devote a whole chapter to them.

PSEUDO WHOLESALERS

These are companies that purport to sell wholesale, but really don't. Pseudo wholesalers will sell to anyone with money. They do not qualify their accounts via resale numbers or other business documentation. Prices will be near or at retail price. We recommend you avoid this kind of supplier unless you know you can turn the product quickly and at a much higher price.

SOURCING FROM CHINA

Sourcing from China (and associated private labeling) is a hot topic in the eCommerce world. Properly done, sourcing products from China gives you the opportunity to add a lot of products to your inventory, but sourcing from China requires product knowledge, shipping knowledge, customs knowledge and superior problem solving skills.

Problems can happen at any part of the process ... from poor quality products to shipping issues to customs issues. You need to have some experience under your belt and really know what you are doing before you jump into China sourcing. Remember: Alibaba and similar sites do not carry name brands. Even if they tell you it's a name brand, chances are it's not.

So please, get some experience with domestic wholesalers before you begin looking into China products, and if you do take the leap, check with your insurance agent or underwriter to make sure you are covered.

Plus

- Wide variety of products
- Good pricing

Minus

- Quality control issues
- Language issues
- Shipping issues
- Customs issues

DROP SHIPPING

Drop shipping is a business model in which the retailer does not keep goods in stock, but instead transfers customer orders and shipment details to either the manufacturer or a wholesaler, who then ships the goods directly to the customer. Drop shipping is all the rage in certain online groups, because it requires very little up-front investment. You don't buy products until they are sold.

We do not recommend drop shipping for Amazon and eBay orders. There is too much risk involved with each transaction, mainly due to slow shipping. Late shipments and items going out of stock without warning are a common problem with drop shippers and are deadly to Amazon and eBay businesses. Both platforms require seller metrics to be superb and drop shipping lowers your chances of remaining a Top Rated Seller or a Featured Merchant.

Plus:
- No cash tied up in inventory

Minus:
- Slow shipping times can lead to unhappy customers
- Products can go out of stock without warning
- You do not have inventory on hand to check quality
- Prices can be higher than traditional wholesale sources

CHAPTER 2 HOMEWORK

- Find one supplier in each of the categories discussed in this chapter

SETTING YOURSELF UP FOR SUCCESS

W e've convinced you to start sourcing wholesale. Before you jump in with both feet, make sure you have everything you need to successfully contact wholesalers. Online sellers are at a disadvantage when contacting wholesalers. You will find that many wholesalers are wary of online businesses, though this is slowly changing. You need to have things in place that will convince them you own a serious business. Put the odds in your favor by following our steps to set up your business.

BUSINESS NAME

You are going to need a business name. A business name is a very personal issue. What you choose depends on your taste, what you sell, and the image you want to project to both wholesalers and to your customers. We strongly suggest that you avoid cutesy names or names that lock you into a single niche, unless it is a large niche. Think about where you want to be in five years or ten years. Don't select a name you'll soon outgrow.

We also suggest you avoid business names that will cause someone to perceive you as a small, hobby business. Would your perception of Amazon be the same if it was called Jeff's Books? Probably not. The first name reads as big and powerful; the second sounds like a small time operation. You want to put all the odds in your favor, and selecting a good business name is a way to get your foot in the door when contacting wholesalers.

Once you have a list of possible names, you need to ask yourself a few questions about the names on your list. Answer these questions for each name and discard the ones that don't make the grade.

Does the name lock in you to a small niche, or a niche you might outgrow? If you are currently selling perfume, you might be tempted to include "perfume" in your store name, but a name like that locks you in a niche. Why not choose a more general name? You could include the word "beauty" or "glamour" in your business name and then not be typecast as a perfume-only seller.

Is the name professional? Select a name that is substantial, a name that oozes quality and stability.

Is the name memorable, or is it common sounding? Will people be able to recall your business name quickly?

Is your business name available as a store name on Amazon and eBay and any other sites you want to sell on? We suggest using the same name on all of your marketplaces.

Can you get .com for the name? Despite what many people will tell you, .com is a must for your business. You may have to alter the name of your business to get the exact .com domain. It is vitally important to have your .com business name; you'll see why further along in this chapter.

Can you get social media pages for that name? You want to be able to promote your business on Facebook, Pinterest, and other social media sites. Make sure your business name is available and lock it in.

BUSINESS REGISTRATION

Once you have selected a business name, your next step is to determine what form you want your business to take. Do you want to operate as a sole proprietor or as an LLC? These are questions you need to ask an attorney or CPA, or both. They can advise you the best way to structure your business for both your current situation and future goals.

We both have structured our businesses as LLCs. Like corporations, LLCs provide their members (owners) protection from liability. This means that members are not personally liable for debts and, often, court judgments incurred by the LLC. Creditors cannot seek the personal assets of the LLC members. It is an important shield not provided in a sole proprietorship or traditional partnership.

Your next step is to register your business with your state. Depending on where you live, you may also be required to register with your county or city. See Appendix B for links to state registration websites. Check your county and city websites for information about registering there.

RESALE NUMBER

Resale numbers are also known as Sales Tax Certificates, Resale Certificates or Tax Exempt Certificates.

Resale numbers are issued by the state, and are used when purchasing items for resale. Most wholesalers require that you provide them with your resale number when you apply to open an account. States that do not have sales tax will provide business certificates that can be used in the same manner. For example, Oregon calls their certificate a Business Registry Resale Certificate. See Appendix C for links to apply for a resale number in your state.

FEDERAL EMPLOYER IDENTIFICATION NUMBER (FEIN, EIN OR TIN)

A FEIN is like a Social Security number for your business. Some wholesalers will ask for an FEIN as part of the business verification process. Marketplaces like Amazon will ask for your FEIN if you are registered as an LLC or a corporation. Contrary to the name, you don't need to have employees to apply for and receive a FEIN. A FEIN is free, and takes just a few minutes to apply for on the IRS web site.

Having a FEIN means that you don't have to give out your personal social security number to vendors. This is a huge security benefit.

DOMAIN NAME AND E-MAIL ACCOUNT

Register the domain name that matches your business name and get the associated e-mail account for your business. Don't use Gmail or other free email accounts. An @gmail.com email address looks unprofessional and may cause wholesalers to question your seriousness as a business. We like GoDaddy for domain registration and other web-related services. Their US-based technical support staff is helpful and knowledgeable.

Once you get your domain name and e-mail address, the next question that comes up is "do I need a web site?"

It depends. If you want to sell products directly from your web site, there are a lot of things to consider. Setting up a site with a shopping cart is the easy part; driving traffic to the site and getting people to buy is the hard part. It is time consuming, and unless you are willing to invest the time in SEO (search engine optimization) and in marketing the web site, you are better off forwarding your domain name to your Amazon and/or eBay stores.

Domain name forwarding lets you automatically direct your domain name's visitors to a different website. So if sometime types in www.yourstore.com, they will be automatically and seamlessly redirected to your Amazon or eBay storefronts (or any other site you choose). We both use forwarding to allow prospective wholesalers to see our marketplace storefronts without having to type in a long, complicated URL.

BUSINESS BANK ACCOUNT

You must have business bank account. Do not use a personal bank account. We know of several cases where banks and credit unions have shut down personal accounts that are used for business. Consistent deposits to a personal bank account from Amazon or PayPal are red flags to banks that business is being conducted through a personal bank account.

Do not commingle business and personal funds. Use your business bank account strictly for business transactions. Commingling funds is a huge red flag to the IRS and puts you on the fast track to an audit.

When you go to the bank to open your account, be sure to take the following:

- Business registration documents from your state
- FEIN
- Driver's license or state issued photo ID
- A second form of ID, such as a passport, Social Security card, student ID card, credit card, or debit card

If you do not have an existing relationship (meaning a personal account, a loan, or a credit card) with a bank, you must go in person to open up your business account. The

Patriot Act mandates this; it is not your bank or banker being difficult.

Talk to your banker about the best way to reduce your bank fees. Automatic transfers from a business checking to a business savings account may be one of many ways you can ensure that your business bank accounts are free. Each bank has different packages and requirements, so be sure to ask your banker.

Take time to build a relationship with your banker; having someone you can call directly when you have questions or problems goes a long way. Build up a relationship and you'll never have to deal with faceless, nameless representatives on a toll-free number. You'll be able to call your banker directly and have him answer your questions, solve a problem, or suggest bank products that can help you build your business.

CREDIT CARD OR DEBIT CARD

A business credit (or debit) card, in your business name, is a must. You need some mechanism to pay wholesalers, and most will take credit or debit cards. As you build up credit and rapport with a wholesaler you can ask for terms, but to open an account, a credit card is a must.

Make sure you take the time to shop around for a card. Costs and benefits for cards vary greatly, and you must weigh the choices to get the card that works best for your business. There are four major credit card companies in the United States: Visa, MasterCard, American Express, and Discover.

Banks, businesses, non-profit groups and other institutions issue cards under these four companies.

When researching credit cards, there are lots of things to consider. Do you want cash back or do you want airline miles? Are you willing to pay an annual fee for a card that includes entry to airline lounges and loss and damage protection? It's a jungle out there and only you can decide what card will work best for you.

While we believe it is important that your business have a credit card, we do not believe that you should go into debt to build your business. We both started with very small amounts of cash and reinvested our earnings to grow our businesses. We believe trying to build your business with credit card debt can be a fatal error. Having debt puts an incredible amount of pressure on a small business, and changes the perception of the way you spend money. In some cases, it will cause a small business to fail.

When one becomes a slave to a lender, we start to make choices that cost us money in the end. The changes in attitude can seem minor at the time, but small things add up to big money. For instance, a small shopping box is needed for an order but the person in debt will use a large box because they have one on hand and don't have the cash to buy a small one. Add up decisions like this every day and pretty soon things are so far gone there is no way to recover.

INSURANCE

Liability insurance is a must. Amazon requires Pro Merchants to name them as an additional insured on a general liability or umbrella insurance policy. If you are not a Pro Merchant, you are required to name Amazon as an additional insured if you exceed their selling threshold (currently $10,000 per month) for three consecutive months.

Whether or not Amazon requires it, we feel very strongly that you should have, at a minimum, a general liability policy. If you store inventory at home or in a warehouse or storage locker, we suggest you have a comprehensive business policy that covers both inventory and liability. A comprehensive business policy can also cover loss of earnings and provide coverage for your computers and other business equipment.

When you look for insurance we suggest you shop around. Ask for recommendations from other online business owners. Ask the agent who covers your home or car if they write commercial business policies. They may be able to help you, or they can refer you to an agent who specializes in business insurance.

The cost of insurance varies from company to company. Where you live, what you sell, and how much you sell are major factors in determining your premium. Other factors include your FICO score, the length of time you have been in business, and the legal structure of your business.

Print out and take the Amazon insurance requirements with you when you meet with the agent. Also take an estimate of your annual sales, and an estimate of the value of the inventory you store at home or in your own warehouse. You don't need to include the value of inventory stored at Amazon's fulfillment centers, as Amazon's insurance covers that inventory.

BUSINESS CARDS

Even in the eCommerce world, you need to have business cards. We use VistaPrint and Moo for our business cards. You can choose from stock designs, or upload your own custom design. If you use VistaPrint, make sure you do not order the free cards with the VistaPrint information on the back. Pay the $10 or so to ensure that your cards are advertising-free.

A business card should contain the company name, your name, the business address and phone number, and your e-mail address. If you have a business logo, use it on your business cards. That's it. Wholesalers don't care about the title you give yourself, and you don't need to add witty taglines or other extraneous information. The purpose of the card is to give the recipient your contact information. Simple and elegant trumps cluttered and overdone every time.

Do invest in decent cardstock. Heavy stock feels better in the hand and subconsciously speaks "money" to whoever handles it. Glossy or matte finish is a matter of taste, and you don't need to spend extra money on metallic inks or other specialty finishes unless it fits your design and your wallet.

We like having a QR Code (Quick Response Code) on the back of our business cards. A QR Code is a two-dimensional barcode that is readable by smartphones. It allows encoding of over 4000 characters into the code. QR Codes may be used to display text to the user, to open a URL, save a contact to the address book or to compose text messages.

There are dozens of free sites that allow you to make your own QR codes. We like The QR Code Generator and QR Stuff to generate QR codes.

CHAPTER 3 HOMEWORK

Set up each of the following for your business:
- Business name
- Business registration with State, County and City
- Resale number
- Domain name and e-mail account
- Business bank account
- Federal Employer Identification Number (FEIN)
- Credit or debit card
- Insurance
- Business cards

CHAPTER 3 RESOURCES

Amazon Insurance Requirements
- http://bit.ly/YUoL4d
- http://bit.ly/YUJapl

GoDaddy
- http://www.godaddy.com

IRS FEIN Registration
- http://1.usa.gov/1tiqN5F

Moo.com
- http://www.moo.com

QR Code Generator
- https://www.the-qrcode-generator.com

QR Stuff
- http://www.qrstuff.com

VistaPrint
- http://www.vistaprint.com

FINDING WHOLESALERS

The question we get asked most often is "Where do I find wholesalers?" That question outnumbers all other questions we receive combined. And funny enough, it's the easiest question to answer. Gone are the days of struggling to make contact with companies through outdated phone books or business registries; with the Internet, millions of products are at your fingertips.

Begin your wholesale search at home. What products do you use regularly? Are there regional or specialty foods that you love? Do you have a hobby that you buy tools or supplies for? Grab a few of those products and start doing your research.

First, take those big name brands and put them back on the shelf. Contacting Mars for a wholesale candy account or Mattel for a toy account isn't the place to begin wholesale sourcing. It's very tempting to start with the big boys, but it is unlikely you will be able to buy from them in a quantity that will allow you to compete on price.

Instead, find products from smaller, niche companies. Then turn over the box or package and look for contact information for the company. Look them up on Google. Check out their web site. You now know where to begin to find products. It really is that simple.

Ask your friends and family for product recommendations. Listen to your friends when they mention a product they love. People make recommendations all the time, even in passing conversation. Once you have the product name, you can then contact the manufacturer. Darla found a Mom and Pop wholesale company simply by talking with a friend about a product she loved. In fact, it was her very first wholesale account!

Don't forget to check out products that your spouse, partner or a child uses. Children in particular can be a huge asset in doing product research. They are on top of trends and what is going to be the next big thing, so take advantage of their knowledge. You might even want to have periodic focus groups with your children and their friends to talk about new products.

Every town, no matter how small, seems to have at least one local manufacturer. Charlene opened a wholesale account with a small specialty sporting goods manufacturer in her little town. It is a matter of keeping your eyes and ears open. Drive around any industrial or commercial area in your hometown, looking for signs, trucks, or whatever other clues you might find. If your town still has a phone book, look through it for possible contacts. Google Local can also be a lead-generating source. Contact the companies that seem promising.

If you are currently selling products that you source from a retail or online source (retail or online arbitrage), contact the manufacturer of those products to see if you can open a wholesale account. Be aware that the prices on small wholesale orders may not be as low as you can find through clearance or other sales, but it is always worth investigating. This is an especially useful tactic with small, niche wholesalers who are new to market and are not yet being sold on Amazon.

As you go through your daily life, you may find that you run across products you admire but, for whatever reason, don't purchase. These products may be something you know little about, or are out of your price range. These are great sourcing opportunities. Investigate them a little bit and see if they will work for your business. Products such as these allow you to stretch by moving into new product lines, and they may also grow your customer base by appealing to a whole new segment of the market.

Stroll the aisles of small stores like gourmet food stores or boutique pet stores with an eye to finding wholesale sources. Look at the product lines the stores carry, and discreetly note the name of the manufacturers that look promising. Be respectful when using retail stores for research … don't make a mess, don't get in the way of other shoppers, and be kind to the sales clerks.

Charlene has been successful finding new wholesalers from ads in trade magazines. A trade magazine is a magazine targeted to people in a specific industry. For example, there are trade magazines for industries as varied as hairdressers and pet stores. Trade magazines contain advertising content centered on the industry in question. These ads may be for specific products, entire product lines, or for distributors. Trade magazines may also contain ads for jobs in the industry, and provide insight into trends in the industry as well.

Most trade magazines are free, providing you meet the criteria set by the publisher. You can find trade magazines at Free Trade Magazine Source, and at TradePub, as well as by doing a Google search.

Trade shows, markets and marts are a huge sourcing opportunity. They are so important that we have devoted Chapter 5 to them.

CHAPTER 4 HOMEWORK

- Find at least three new wholesale sources
- Contact the wholesalers and ask how to apply for a new account
- Find a trade magazine in an industry you are interested in and subscribe to it

CHAPTER 4 RESOURCES

Free Trade Magazine Source
- http://www.freetrademagazinesource.com

Google Local
- https://plus.google.com/local

TradePub
- http://www.tradepub.com

WORKING WITH WHOLESALERS

Whether your initial contact with a wholesaler is through email, a phone call, or a trade show, it can be a nerve-wracking experience, especially if you are new to the game. Learning the terminology and basic practices used in the wholesale sector can go a long way toward easing the way.

When you first contact a wholesaler, they will generally ask for some basic information about your business. Besides the contact information for you and your business, they will most likely ask for your state resale number. Some will ask for your FEIN. And some will ask for references.

In general, wholesalers will ask you for two kinds of references: trade references and credit references. Trade references are other suppliers you do business with. For example, if you are contacting a grocery company for a wholesale account, you may be asked to provide trade references in the grocery sector. If you are new to wholesale sourcing and don't have references in the sector, be honest and tell the prospective supplier that you are just beginning to expand into that area.

Credit references are any companies that you do business with. It could be UPS, your cell phone provider, or other vendors you use in business. Credit references are used to determine whether the company should extend credit terms to you. If you plan to pay for your orders with a credit card, you can just note that information in the "credit reference" section of the application.

There can be confusion and crossover between trade and credit references. For example, that grocery company you buy from can be both a trade and a credit reference. Don't get bogged down about references ... if you have a question about what kind of reference the wholesaler is looking for, just ask them.

Don't rule out asking for terms when you open a new wholesale account. Terms can offer you the opportunity to use someone else's money (meaning the supplier) for a certain period of time before you have to pay for the product. For example, 30-day terms means you have 30 days from the invoice date to pay for your order. In a perfect world you would have sold those products in the 30 days and have the money to pay for them (and some profit) in your bank account when the invoice comes due.

Some suppliers will ask that your first few orders be prepaid (usually by credit card) and then they will extend terms to you. The ideal situation is a supplier that offers 30-day terms, and then allows you to pay the invoice on a credit card ... which mean you can have another month or so before you actually have to pay for the product. You also gain the benefits associated with the credit card, whether they are points or cash back.

You need to ask the wholesaler about lead times for products, especially new-to-market products. Regular stock items may ship to you in a day or two, but new products can have lead times that range from weeks to months. Both Charlene and Darla ordered products at different trade shows last February that had six-month lead times. You need to factor lead times in to your overall buying plan. If you buy too many products with long lead times you may be sitting around for months with no products to sell.

Before you place an order, you need to be clear about who pays for shipping the products to you. Do you pay, or does the supplier pay? Or do you pay until your order reaches a certain threshold, at which time the supplier pays, or offers a discount? These are all common scenarios, so you need to make sure you know which scenario you will be working under so you can factor that into your pricing.

Wholesalers may not always offer the best deals on shipping. This is especially true of small wholesalers who may not have a lot of experience in shipping. If a shipping charge seems to be out of line, ask them to double-check the rates. Get the weight and dimensions and check shipping charges on your own account. If you can ship cheaper on your own account, ask them if they would use your shipping label to ship your order. You can send them a PDF of the shipping label, which they can print and affix to your order.

You will inevitably be faced with items that are damaged in shipment. Even with the best packing, damage happens. If you spot damage to items in your shipment, stop unpacking and grab your camera. Take a few shots of the box, and the damaged items, as they are unpacked. You don't need to go overboard, but pictures make for faster resolution of any issues.

Depending on the company, there are a few things that can happen when you report items damaged in shipment. If the items are inexpensive, the company may say you can just keep them and they will credit your account. Or they may offer you a percentage discount off the price of the items if you want to keep them. Fifteen percent is a common percentage. Only you can determine whether this is a big enough discount for you to keep the items and try to sell them. If the damage is only to the packaging, this may work.

Lastly, the company may ask you to return the items for a credit to your account. In most cases, they will pay for return shipping. They may send you a call tag (prepaid shipping label) from UPS, or they may ask you to return the items at your expense and they will credit you with the shipping you paid. When returning items to a wholesaler, you will be provided a Return Merchandise Authorization (RMA) number. This number identifies the shipment to the wholesaler so your account can be properly credited. Be sure this number is on the outside of the box and on any paperwork inside the box.

You may also find that a shipment is short one or more items. If this happens, contact the company immediately. Though short shipments can be a "he said, she said" situation, you'll find that the vast majority of wholesalers know mistakes happen in their fulfillment department and will act quickly to make the situation right. Larger companies have systems in place that can accurately compute what the weight a box should be based on what is packed in it. This makes it easy to resolve shipments that are short. Either way, do not hesitate to contact the company should you receive a short shipment. You are entitled to get what you paid for.

As you gain experience in working with wholesalers, you will gain confidence in your abilities to negotiate a deal that works for you and for the wholesaler. Remember, wholesalers need you to sell their products. And while some wholesalers are gun-shy about doing business with online retailers, there are many more who will welcome your business.

When you are beginning to build a relationship with a wholesaler, don't be afraid to ask for what you want. Do you want a shipping discount? Are you looking for a price break for a certain quantity? Don't be afraid to ask; all they can say is no.

Many online retailers have built relationships with wholesalers that include having the wholesalers ship products directly to warehouse fulfillment centers. While this may seem like the holy grail of wholesale sourcing, it is a process that is fraught with issues. We recommend that you never have your initial order from a wholesaler shipped directly to a fulfillment center. You need to see the product. You need to make sure you are getting what you were promised. You need to see how it is packaged and what prep is required. You need to make sure the wholesaler ships accurately and ships orders complete.

If you are comfortable with the way a wholesaler ships their products to you, you can then approach them about shipping directly to a fulfillment center. Some wholesalers are open to doing this, others will refuse. Some wholesalers are afraid of the process. Some don't want to do anything that might disrupt their standard workflow. Whether the refusal is based in fact or fear, respect their wishes. Pushing too hard on this issue may alienate the wholesaler.

CHAPTER 5 HOMEWORK:

- Review the glossary so you become familiar with the terminology wholesalers use
- Contact seven new wholesalers a week (one a day) for four weeks

TRADE SHOWS, MARKETS AND MARTS

Traditionally, trade shows are annual or semi-annual events. They are temporary, short-term events, usually running one to four days. Trade shows can be held in the same location, year after year, or they can move around the country.

Markets and marts contain showrooms, and are open year-round, at a permanent, fixed location. Temporary exhibitors (called temporaries) may also set up at a market during specified periods of time.

Whether you choose to attend a trade show or a market, the information presented here will help you make the most of your time and money at the show. Most of the information we present here will apply to both trade shows and markets. Where there are clear differences between the two, we will point out and explain the differences and how they might affect you as a buyer.

FINDING TRADE SHOWS

Trade shows are Charlene's favorite way to source products. Imagine hundreds or thousands of wholesalers, all under one roof. Sourcing heaven! Trade shows put you at an advantage in the marketplace because you'll have the chance to see products before they come to market. You can also spot trends and meet vendors to strike deals in person. Some trade shows also offer classes, seminars and workshops to help you grow your business.

Finding trade shows is easy. The hard part is deciding which ones will fit your business. If you sell in a niche, it becomes easier, as many trade shows focus on products for a particular niche. Examples of these types of shows are the National RV Trade Show and the National Hardware Show.

Generalist shows, which carry a wide range of products, include shows like ASD in Las Vegas and the Mega Show in Hong Kong. Generalist shows are especially useful if you do not sell in a niche or are looking to expand into new niches.

The first place to look for trade shows is on the web. Our favorite source is Trade Show News Network. Trade Show News Network allows you to search for shows by date, by location, or by vendor or product type. If you sign up for their mailing list, you'll receive notices about upcoming shows that meet your search criteria.

You can also find trade shows through trade organizations such as Outdoor Retailer or the Craft and Hobby Association, or through trade publications, magazines, or by being on wholesaler mailing lists.

Your local Chamber of Commerce will have information about trade shows in your area. You can also contact local convention centers and conference organizers for information about upcoming shows in your area.

When you are deciding which trade shows you want to attend, keep in mind that there are three basic kinds of trade shows, and entrance requirements will differ between them:

- Shows like Craft and Hobby Association Mega Show, where you must be a member of the sponsoring trade organization to attend the show
- Shows like Outdoor Retailer Show, where you must qualify to attend the show by providing a certain number of wholesale invoices in the niche, as well as a business card, and, in some cases, a voided check from your business bank account
- Shows like ASD, where anyone with general business documents can attend. These documents typically include a resale certificate and a business card

FINDING MARKETS AND MARTS

Since markets and marts are year round events and stay in the same location, finding them is pretty simple. A Google search of "wholesale marts" or "wholesale markets" will turn up dozens of them for you.

REGISTERING FOR A TRADE SHOW OR MARKET

Once you have decided on what show you want to attend, you need to register for the show. Most shows will allow online registration, so check the show's web site. We strongly urge you to register for the show as soon as you decide you want to attend. Some shows, like Outdoor Retailer, have an in-depth vetting process, and you do not want to be denied entry to the show because you have not submitted the proper documents. Other shows are far more casual, but by being registered ahead of time, there won't be any nasty surprises when you get to the show.

ADVANCE PLANNING

Attending a show takes advance planning and organization. You need to be prepared! You also need to make sure you have set yourself up for success at the show. Here's what we suggest you bring to the show:

- Show registration confirmation and/or badges. Charlene keeps a copy of these documents in Evernote in case the hard copies are lost. Darla labels the email confirmation and archives it.
- Copies of your resale certificate. Many vendors will want a copy of this document to place an order. Bring plenty of copies and put a copy in Evernote, too.
- Business cards. Take more than you think you'll need. Business cards are cheap and you'll be giving out a lot of them.

- Folders to organize fliers, business cards, catalogs, etc. Charlene likes Smead poly envelopes.
- Note-taking stuff. Use whatever is most efficient for you, whether if be a smartphone, tablet, or pencil and paper. Darla likes the Cambridge Notebook because it has a folder in the front of it where you can store your sales tax certificate.

Once you have registered for the show, check to see if the show has a planning app for your smartphone. These apps typically include maps of the venue, workshop schedules, and exhibitor lists with search capabilities. The best ones allow you to make appointments with vendors you really want to spend time with. Download the app and become familiar with its capabilities before you leave for the show.

TRAVELING TO THE SHOW

Unless the show is in your hometown, you need to get there and have a place to stay once you arrive. If the show is close, you can drive, but in most cases you'll need to fly to get to the show. Charlene has logged over a million miles in the air and has some suggestions for getting the best deal on your airfare and hotel.

Many shows will have made agreements with travel agencies to offer air/hotel packages for attendees. While these packages can be a good deal, you must shop around to make sure you know what you are getting and it suits your needs.

Join the membership rewards program for all of the major airlines and hotel chains. Being a member of a hotel reward program can be the difference between getting a reservation and finding no room at the inn. In addition, membership in these programs can lead to upgrades and free room nights.

Find a good travel agent. An experienced travel agent is worth their weight in gold. A travel agent can find hidden deals, and a good agent has resources civilians don't have. For example, Charlene's travel agent follows her trips in real time. While on the way to a trade show, a delay occurred while she was on the first flight of a three-flight trip. The second flight had been delayed, which meant she would miss her last connection. Her agent rebooked her on another flight while she was in the air and she made her connection. Internet airfare sites can't do this for you.

If possible, stay on the concierge level of your hotel. Concierge levels often provide free breakfast and evening drinks and appetizers, which can cut your food bill dramatically. Also, many concierge levels provide soft drinks, juices and bottled water throughout the day. Take advantage of what is offered, but please, don't empty the refrigerator. Take only what you can use.

PHYSICAL COMFORT AT THE SHOW

Attending a trade show is hard on your body. Your comfort begins with some organization and advance preparation. Here are some hints to get you started:

Use a rolling bag, if show regulations allow. Catalogs and price lists get heavy fast! Charlene and Darla both swear by Zuca bags. Not only are they fantastic for carrying all the paperwork and samples you accumulate, they also have a seat built into the top. Chairs can be hard to come by at trade shows and having your seat with you at all times can be a lifesaver.

Take your own water and snacks. Convention center prices for food and drink can take a big bite out of your budget. Save money and time by bringing your own. If you are staying on the concierge floor of your hotel you can grab some water there. If you aren't, find a convenience store and stock up for the show.

Wear comfortable shoes and dress in layers. This isn't the time or the place to break in a new pair of shoes. Wear a broken-in, comfortable pair that will allow you to be on your feet for eight to 10 hours. Convention centers tend to be over-cooled, so dress in layers so you can adjust your wardrobe to keep yourself comfortable. Business casual is the recommended dress code ... please, no shorts and cheap flip flops, no matter what the weather. Present yourself in a professional manner so vendors will take you seriously.

Trade shows are crowded, busy, hectic places. Keep your wallet or your purse in a safe place. Women should consider a cross-body bag so you won't have to set down your bag to inspect products. Men should carry their wallets in their front pockets. A rubber band around the wallet will make it harder for someone to get it out of your pocket without your knowledge.

Check photography rules and regulations. Some shows prohibit photographs and will confiscate cameras or smartphones if you break this rule.

HITTING THE SHOW FLOOR

Before you head out to the show, find the list of vendors, either on the show website or on the show app. Start researching the products they carry. While nothing is as good as seeing the product lines in person, a little advance research can help you rule out vendors that you can skip as well as those that are a must to see.

Can you scan products at trade shows and markets? We have never had an issue scanning at trade shows (versus markets and marts, where scanning is often frowned upon). We are discreet about it, and we try to scan a few products before we start a conversation with a salesperson. Knowing a few things about the line before starting a discussion can help you ask the right questions.

We both believe the New Exhibitor (Temporaries) area is the best place to start at a show. In many cases, the early bird gets the worm. Those who find a new product line first are at a huge advantage over others. Being first to find a new product offers the opportunity to get an exclusive agreement (see Chapter Ten for more on exclusives) as well as be in on any advertising and other marketing the manufacturer does for the product.

Schedule appointments with vendors ahead of time, if possible. If the show has a smartphone app, look to see if there is a way to schedule an appointment in advance through the app. Having an appointment will ensure that you have the undivided attention of the salesperson ... they won't be trying to juggle three or four people at one time. Be respectful of the vendors and only schedule appointments with vendors you are serious about working with.

Watch for show specials from vendors you already use. Taking advantage of show specials from existing vendors can save you enough to pay for your travel and hotel expenses. Show specials can vary, from free shipping to a percentage off of an order. Some vendors are especially creative in their discount structure and offer decreasing discount amounts as the show progresses. The discount might be 15% on orders placed on day one, 10% on orders placed on day two, and 5% on orders placed on day three.

WHAT DO I ASK?

So you explored the show floor, and have found a vendor that has products you are interested in. What should you ask them? What do you need to know before you make a decision about the product line? These are some of the basic questions we ask prospective vendors:

- Do they sell to Amazon?

- Do they sell on Amazon themselves?
- What is the minimum opening order?
- What is the minimum reorder?
- Do they enforce MAP pricing?
- Do they offer terms? How do they want an order paid for?
- Where is the order shipped from?
- Who pays shipping? Is there an order level that will get you free shipping?
- Will they accept stock back if it doesn't sell?
- Can you get an Amazon exclusive?
- Do they provide stock photos, videos, and other marketing assistance?
- Do they have a YouTube channel?

PLACING ORDERS

Be very careful placing orders for new products at the show. If you are new to the show scene, be doubly careful. We both have a basic rule: do not order new products while on the show floor. It's very easy to get swept up in the excitement of the show and order products before you have done your due diligence. You need to be able to think clearly, run the numbers, and do your homework before you place an order. It's hard to do that amid the excitement of the show floor.

Most vendors will honor show specials for a set period of time after the show, so you don't need to be in a rush to order. If they don't volunteer information about extending a show special, don't be afraid to ask. Tell them you need time to think and would like to place an order after you get back home.

The exception to the rule about not ordering at a show doesn't apply to existing vendors and product lines. If you have a winning product line, reorder at the show to take advantage of any show specials that are being offered. Charlene writes orders for existing lines before she leaves for the show so it only takes a few minutes to submit the order.

Listen more than you speak. In addition to listening to salespeople you are working with, keep your ears open to conversations happening around you. A snippet of overhead information may be just the lead you need to snag a great deal.

While you have to keep your ears open, don't be afraid to ask questions about products. And don't be afraid to ask for what you want from vendors. Is the minimum opening order too high? Ask if they can make an exception for your first order. Want to negotiate a better price on a large order? Ask. The worst they can say is "No". Anything in business is negotiable but you have to come to the table with a clear idea of what you want and what you are willing to give up to strike the deal.

Don't turn down any freebies and samples from vendors. Vendors account for these giveaways in their show budgets as a way to draw attention to their products. Don't be afraid to take advantage of them. And be sure you enter all show drawings and giveaways. You never know what you might win!

NETWORKING AT THE SHOW

Many trade shows offer group meals and seminars. No matter how tired you are, make sure to attend a few seminars and group meals. Do your homework and target industry leaders and contacts you want to meet. Spend some time each day circulating and schmoozing. Time spent networking can pay off in deals that don't make it to the show floor ... many great deals are done over dinner or drinks.

When you finally catch up with a person you wanted to meet, ask them to join you off the show floor, if possible. It's quieter and easier to have a conversation. Offer to buy them a cup of coffee to break the ice. If that person is an industry leader, you may only have a few moments to make an impression before they have to move on, so make the most of it. Be clear in your own mind as to why you wanted to speak with them.

Be open and friendly to everyone. Speak to as many people as you can while waiting in lines. You never know, that person standing next to you might be a great contact.

Have a good quote or two in the back of your mind in case a reporter or producer approaches you. The last trade show Charlene attended was covered by the Today show, so you never know what opportunities you may come across.

MORE ABOUT MARKETS AND MARTS

A market or mart has similarities to a trade show. Vendors are there to sell products to you. However, marts work a bit differently than trade shows in some key areas, which we will cover. Attending a mart can be fun, but it can also be overwhelming. It's OK to be afraid, but don't let that fear control you. And finally, remember that you are a legitimate business and deserve to be there as much as anyone else in that mart.

A mart might remind you of sourcing products at a combined Macy's and Hallmark store. You'll find product categories such as home and kitchen goods, baby, toys, gourmet foods, handbags, shoes, clothing and more at a mart. A mart is not for everyone, but most of them have enough product lines that most people find it well worth their time to attend. The exceptions include niche sellers like Charlene, who find that trade shows targeting her niche are a better use of her time and money. Darla, who sells a much broader range of products, has huge success at marts.

If you can find someone to be your mentor for your first trip to a mart, you will find it incredibly helpful. Having someone who knows the ropes can save you hours of frustration. Just remember your mentor is there to do business as well and will have to break away after they get you rolling to conduct their own business. A mentor can be that key person you need to ensure a smooth introduction to vendors at the mart, so do some networking and see if you can find a mentor to help you out your first trip to market.

Scanning products is not encouraged at a mart, and in some cases it is frowned upon. This unwritten policy may change over the course of time as vendors are becoming more open to online sellers. We encourage you to take time to people-watch for a couple hours to see how it all flows at that particular mart.

On your first day at the mart, do not buy anything. Collect catalogs and take them back to your hotel room and research the products. Most vendors understand it's your first day and will give you the information you need to make a decision. Just say, "Can I please get a catalog? It's my first day here, I'll be back tomorrow."

If you are attending your first show, we encourage to be guarded and think clearly so you don't get taken advantage of by the sales reps in the showrooms. Don't misunderstand; the reps are all legitimate, but they do not always have your best interest at heart. You need to realize they want to sell products and will do what it takes to do so. So take time to walk through each aisle (without walking into a booth unless it screams your name) and see the product, collect a catalog and ask for your area's sales rep and contact information. Do the research and make it a priority to build relationships with your local sales reps. See chapter 7 for more information about sales reps.

One thing you will notice at a mart is that one rep may carry as many as 20 different product lines. This can get a bit confusing as you try to keep track of who sells what. We recommend taking a notebook and writing down all information you can get from a rep about all of the products they represent. Charlene uses Evernote to do this; Darla likes a physical notebook. It doesn't matter how you record the details, the important things is that you have the information. You will be amazed at all the product opportunities one sales rep can show you. You might start out talking to a rep about baby products and end up looking at a line of kitchen items.

IN CONCLUSION

While attending a trade show or market can seem overwhelming, if you follow the suggestions in this chapter, you'll soon feel comfortable at a show and you will find that they are unrivaled in their ability to bring together hundreds or thousands of vendors to you, all in one place.

CHAPTER 6 HOMEWORK

- Find three trade shows and three markets you have an interest in attending and apply to attend them
- If any of the shows require documentation such as invoices to attend, put together the required information
- Join hotel and airline rewards programs
- Find a good travel agent
- Put together your show survival kit

CHAPTER 6 RESOURCES

Evernote
- https://evernote.com

Trade Show News Network

- http://www.tsnn.com

Zuca

- http://www.zuca.com

CLOSING THE DEAL

W e've asked Ron Davison to contribute a chapter to this book, focusing on his specialty: doing the deal. We're happy he agreed to write this chapter and that we can share this "Guide to Establishing a Relationship with a New Supplier" with you.

INTRODUCTION

So picture this: you're at a trade show, looking for things to sell on your Amazon storefront. You're going from booth to booth, looking at exhibitors and collecting a bag full of brochures and business cards, and hopefully picking up some freebies along the way. You turn a corner and spot something that genuinely interests you. You've never seen it before, and it's fresh and innovative. Your gut feeling tells you that this is a winner.

You step away, pull out your smartphone, and search the Internet for the product. You find few, if any, results, and your heartbeat quickens as you realize that no one's selling it yet! You know that you've got a golden opportunity here.

You can get in on a product line that no one's selling yet, and better yet, maybe even be the only one that will sell it. But you're wracked with doubt, thinking something like:

- He'll never sell to me.
- She's not going to be interested in doing business with us.
- They're too big to want to do business with me.

Stop. Wait. Think again. Remember that vendors need retailers more than retailers need vendors; you can always go find another product to sell, but what are they going to do if no one buys from them? So, bearing this in mind, you realize that you've got an opportunity here. Let's face it: you've got nothing to lose except a little time. So, make sure that that time is not wasted. Let's break down what you're trying to achieve:

- You want to sell this product on Amazon.
- If at all possible, you want to be the only seller of this product on Amazon.

In order to do this, you've got to get the seller to agree to sell to you (and hopefully, only you). Here's how you're going to achieve it.

FACT FINDING

Before you buy a car, you take it for a test drive. Before you buy a pair of shoes, you try them on. And if the opportunity presents itself, before you buy an ice cream cone, you ask for a sample to taste. It stands to reason that you would do the same with a product that you want to carry. At this point, you've got to not just slow down, but come to a complete stop.

Kevin O'Leary of Shark Tank fame is fond of saying: "Here's how I think of my money: as soldiers. I send them out to war everyday. I want them to take prisoners and come home, so there's more of them." One can interpret this as remembering that the best-case scenario is that by buying this product, you're going to tie up working capital for at least a month or two before seeing a return. Ask yourself the following:

- Do I like this product?
- Can I devote enough time to this product to make it successful?
- Can I make money selling this product, and if so, is this product going to give me the best return on my investment?

If the answer to any of the proceeding questions is no, then don't waste your time, or that of the exhibitor. There's simply no point talking to them. Find something else that you can wholeheartedly get behind. But if the answer to all three is yes, then proceed.

THE INTRODUCTION

This is important. Remember that the exhibitor is going to be at best, distracted, or at worst, completely frazzled. You've got to get his attention, hold it, and get your point across succinctly. So, it's good to go in prepared.

It is likely that there is more than one person working the booth. Assuming that this is the case, the exhibitors will likely have business cards somewhere in the booth. Find them. How many people have business cards there? Grab one of each, and read them. Look at the people working the booth. How many of them are there? Can you put names to people at this point? It's pretty easy if there are two business cards, one with a man's name and one with a woman's, and you can see one man and one woman running the stand.

According to the business cards, who has what position in the company? Let's say that, you've determined that Jane Doe is the owner, and John Smith is the marketing executive. Here's the ideal situation: Talk to someone other than the owner first, and preferably, someone of some importance and seniority within the company. This allows you to do some serious fact-finding and get some questions answered prior to talking to the owner.

Ask the following questions:

- Where is it made?
- How long do they take to produce?
- How many do you have in stock?
- How long will it take to fulfill orders I place?
- What's your return policy?
- What's your warranty policy?
- What's your RMA procedure?

Ask anything else you can think of. At this point, there are no dumb questions.

By doing this, when you do talk to the owner, you will have some knowledge of the product, the company, their policies, and (hopefully) the owner. So, assuming that the booth is relatively busy and Jane is occupied, you're going talk to John first, using the talking points in outlined in Chapter Six.

With these questions answered you are now in a position to proceed, assuming that you still feel good about the prospect of carrying the product. As Charlene and Darla said in Chapter 6, don't feel that you have to rush in to committing to buy, but now is the time to talk to the main decision maker, who we are going to assume is the owner. Here's how I do it:

"Hi Jane, I'm Ron. It's a pleasure to meet you. I love your product line, and I'd like to talk to you for a few minutes. Is now a bad time?"

Stop and look at the previous paragraph. It's simple, straightforward, and takes less than ten seconds to say. I've deliberately said; "Is now a bad time?" as opposed to "Is now a good time?" People's knee jerk reaction when asked a question is to give a "no" response – think about the last time you walked into a store, looking to buy something. Maybe it was a pair of shoes, or a TV. You've been in the store 30 seconds when a salesperson asks you "Can I help you find anything?" and before you've even thought of it, you've replied, "No, I'm just looking." Three minutes later, you've got questions, and you're looking for someone to help you.

Bearing this in mind, I deliberately structured that question to elicit a "no" response, because it gets the no out of the way. Most importantly, it will make the Jane stop and think about what you've just asked, and get her to be honest with herself. Assuming that you've got the no that you want (which means that Jane has time to talk to you), it's time to press on.

When you're talking to a vendor, remember that you're attempting to enter into what will hopefully be a lasting, mutually beneficial relationship. And as countless relationship experts have stated, be honest and be yourself. Meaning: don't present yourself as something you're not.

Tell Jane that you've been talking to John, and that based on what you've learned, you'd like to sell her product line. Gauge her reaction – she'll probably be receptive, and if she is, press on with some details about you, your operation, and what you want to achieve by working with her. While you're getting to know Jane, consider whether or not you'd enjoy working with her – if you wouldn't, then doing business is going to be difficult. If things are going well, you've got to make a judgment call at this point:

- Are things going well?
- Do you still want to do business with Jane?
- Are you completely confident in your decision to carry this product range?
- Can you commit to doing a deal right now?
- Does the time feel right to continue the conversation?

If the answer to any of these questions is no, then at an opportune moment, thank Jane for her time, present her with one of your business cards, and move on. But if the answer to all of the above is yes, then it is time to ...

MAKE THE PROPOSITION

So, you've decided that the time is right to make Jane an offer. It's very important at this time that you know what you want, you know what you bring to the table, and you are able to communicate it effectively.

You're about to ask for an exclusive. This is something that vendors are naturally wary of, because on the surface it may seem to them that they're going to sell less on Amazon, because they can only sell to you. It's your job to quickly put aside this notion, and show Jane that not only is she going to sell just as many units by selling only to you, she's going to spend less time and effort too. Consider the following benefits that you can offer Jane:

- Only have to deal with one company–and one person–you
- Fewer outbound shipments
- More predictable inventory flow
- Less invoicing, bookkeeping, and following up on accounts
- Less policing of Minimum Advertised Price and Manufacturer's Suggested Retail Price
- No need to continuously monitor listing quality
- More streamlined logistics

- Brand protection (less risk of counterfeit or misrepresented products)

OBJECTIONS YOU MAY ENCOUNTER

If I sell just to you, I'll sell fewer units.

To understand the root of this objection and understand what Jane is thinking, flip it around: "If I sell to more people, I'll sell more units." At first glance that seems pretty reasonable, but consider this: In any mall food court there's only one McDonald's. Let's say that the restaurant sells 1000 hamburgers a day, because that's how many the public wants to buy. Opening a second McDonald's in the same food court won't mean that the second restaurant will also sell 1000 hamburgers a day – instead, each McDonalds will probably sell 500 hamburgers a day, because that's the demand for hamburgers. It's the same with Amazon as a marketplace. There are a finite number of widgets that will sell on Amazon on any given day, whether the number is 10, 100, or 1000. All other things being equal, doubling the number of Amazon sellers of that widget will halve the number of widgets that each seller will sell.

So it doesn't matter how many Amazon sellers Jane sells to, once the market finds its level, she will sell the same number of units that will ultimately be purchased on Amazon.

Knowing this, you can use the McDonald's analogy in your ongoing discussion with Jane, and overcome her objection to granting you exclusive rights to sell on Amazon.

I don't have time to deal with this right now.

This is not actually an objection; it's an opportunity for further discussion. What Jane is actually saying is that she thinks that the necessary steps for entering into an exclusive agreement with you will be complicated. Your task here is to reassure Jane that doing business with you will be easy.

We don't want our products to be sold on Amazon, or we don't want our products to be sold online.

This is an emotional objection as opposed to a logical one. It's important to understand the basis for the objection: fear. Jane is afraid that there will be negative consequences for allowing her products to be sold in an online marketplace. Your task here is to reassure Jane that there are no downsides to partnering with you. She may be concerned that having her products sold on Amazon (or online in general) will cheapen her brand, alienating her other retailers, because she has the misconception that all online shopping is "discount" shopping. At this point, press for specifics, and listen very carefully to the answers, because without her realizing it, Jane is about to give you the tools you need to win her over. Some sample questions you could ask are:

- Have you ever had any of your products sold online?
- If so, what worked well?
- What didn't work well?
- If not, why not?
- Have you sold your own products online?
- If so, what worked well?

- What didn't work well?
- What did you enjoy about selling online?
- What did you hate about selling online?
- Do you shop online?
- If so, what do you enjoy about shopping online?
- If not, why not?
- What negative experiences have you had while shopping online?

Look at the questions above. Consider all the possible answers to each question, and then think about how you can discuss each of the answers in a light that favors you and your business.

Giving you an exclusive will annoy my brick and mortar stores.

Begin by asking Jane the following questions:

- How many stores are you in?
- Which states are you in?

Chances are that the product range is not sold in all states, let alone every city in the USA. If someone could buy the item in a store today for $19.95, why would they buy it online for $19.95 plus shipping, and have to wait for it to be delivered? It's because not everyone has access to a wide variety of retail stores. Or they might not have the means to get out to stores. Offering the product range for sale on Amazon gives people who can't go to a brick and mortar store the opportunity to buy the product. If the product is sold at the recommended retail price both online and in stores, then there is no conflict of interest and little chance of annoying your brick and mortar stores.

Do you have your own website?

This question is not an objection, it is an opportunity. Jane is starting to embrace to the idea of doing business with you. Your internal reaction at this point is going to probably be "Oh crap – I don't have a website. I'm toast." This is not the case. Why don't you have a website? It's probably because you don't need one. If you needed a website to sell, you'd have one. You have made a business decision to utilize Amazon to market your products, and handle the fulfillment and customer service.

I believe that competition is healthy … you shouldn't have a monopoly.

Amazon is not the entire Internet. It is not the only place to buy products online. According to Quora.com, there are over 100,000 eCommerce sites in the USA alone. As I said earlier in this chapter, being the only seller of a product on Amazon is like being the only McDonald's restaurant in a single mall food court. It is not like forbidding any company besides McDonald's from selling a hamburger in the USA. The product exclusives I have on Amazon still face plenty of healthy competition from other eCommerce sites worldwide.

Why don't I just sell on Amazon myself? Why do I need you?

This could make your blood run cold, but don't let it. Instead, realize at this point that Jane has come to the conclusion that having her product line sold on Amazon is a good idea. This works to your advantage, and you just have to reinforce whose role is what. At this point, in your own words, tell Jane that in order to answer that question, you need to ask her three questions:|

- How long have you been doing this?
- How many hours a week do you spend on your business?
- What are your plans for the business?

Of course, it's impossible to predict exactly what kind of reply you're going to get, but here are a few scenarios:

Scenario One:

Jane has been in the industry for eight years. She spends 40-50 hours a week on her business, selling wholesale to brick and mortar stores. She hopes to expand the business by increasing overall sales, and she has considered developing a website to sell to the public.

What you've learned:

Jane has considerable experience in her field. She is obviously good at what she does, and it has taken her time to gain this experience. She is open to the idea of online sales, but is already working full time on the business.

How to use these facts to your advantage:

Jane is already very busy. It would not appear that she has the time to develop and market her own website. The most valuable thing you can offer her is rapid expansion into an additional marketplace.

"Jane, you've been doing this for a while and clearly you're doing well, but you're already working full time, and then some! You also mentioned that you're going to be even busier in the future as you expand the business. You've worked hard to develop your business, and you're good at it. But you clearly don't have the additional time it takes to sell on Amazon. I've got a lot of experience selling on Amazon, and it took me a lot of time to develop those skills. I know that by working together, we can both be successful. What are your thoughts?"

Scenario Two:

Jane was in brick and mortar retail sales for several years before becoming a stay at home mom. Now that her children are in school, she's getting back into business for herself, and has been doing this for less than a year. She's currently spending about three hours a day on the business, except when she's at trade shows. She hopes that she will be able to expand the business to supplement the family income.

What you've learned:

Jane has some prior experience in her field, and is hard at work re-entering the field. She has a family, and by the sound of things, not too much free time. She wants to grow the business, but her time is split between the needs of her family, and her business.

How to use these facts to your advantage:

Jane has prior experience in retail, but no online sales experience. Her time is extremely limited, because her time is split between work and home. You have the ability to maximize her return on the time she invests in her business. By partnering with you, Jane gains an ally with current online market experience that can help her grow her business. The most valuable thing you can offer her is your experience.

"Jane, I think it's great that you're getting back into retail. You're wearing many hats right now – entrepreneur, business lady, and mom rolled into one. Because of this, I know your time is limited. I can help grow your business by taking care of all sales on

Amazon, which frees up your time so you can focus on other areas of your business. How does that sound?"

Scenario Three:

Jane has been working in wholesale for over thirty years. She's spending at least 50 hours a week on the business. She'd like to streamline the operation to enable her to take it easier.

What you've learned:

Jane has considerable experience in her field, and would well be considered an expert. She's working very long hours, and is looking to find ways of working fewer hours.

How to use these facts to your advantage:

By partnering with you, Jane can deal with just one Amazon seller as opposed to many. The immediate benefit to working with just you is spending less time taking orders, shipping orders, and collecting payments. The long-term benefit that is often overlooked is that Jane will spend considerably less time checking Amazon to make sure her product is being properly represented, portrayed, and priced. Jane is working a lot, and so the most valuable thing you can offer her is saving time by partnering with you.

"Jane, you're clearly an expert when it comes to wholesaling! You've worked extremely hard to build your business. You mentioned earlier that you were looking for ways to lessen your workload. I know that by us partnering, I can make your life easier, save you a lot of time, and generate significant sales revenue for you. It'll be a win-win situation for us both. What questions do you have for me?"

These are just a few examples, but they illustrate the point that you can talk to a person who has been business three months or for thirty years. Try this exercise: write out list of your skills, and why your business is an attractive proposition to partner with. When you're talking to a prospective partner, listen to what they're saying, and think about how you can match it to items on this list.

CLOSING THE DEAL

At this point, due to your extensive preparation, fact-finding, and asking of pertinent questions, you've made a great first impression. You've fielded Jane's questions well, and have given a good accounting of yourself. Jane has agreed to move forward with your dealer application, and to talk further about an exclusivity agreement. So what happens next? It is imperative to make sure that you and Jane exchange contact information. Of course, you swap business cards, but I like to take it a step further.

My business cards have a QR code on the back of them that, when scanned, saves my contact information to a smartphone. When presenting my business card, I point out the QR code on the back. It's a great talking point. If the recipient of one of my cards hasn't already downloaded a QR code reader, I know that they will, just to try it out! You can create and download your own QR code for free at QRstuff.com, then have them printed on the back of your business cards.

To capture business card information, I use an app on my iPhone called Business Card Reader Pro to immediately import a printed business card to my phone's address book.

No matter what mobile platform you're on, there are many similar tools available, and you can choose one that will work for you and your budget.

So, now that you've ensured that you've both got each other's information, tell Jane that you will send her a brief email later that day, thank her for her time, wish her luck with the trade show, and exit confidently with your head held high.

FOLLOW UP

Go grab a drink or a snack, and while everything is fresh in your mind, pull out your smartphone, tablet or laptop and compose a brief email to Jane:

Dear Jane,

It was great getting to know you at the trade show today. I never thought I'd meet a fellow aficionado of Tuvan throat singing at a trade show!

I just wanted to say again how impressed I am with your product range, and I am looking forward to further discussing selling it on our Amazon storefront. Please contact me when you're home from the trade show and we'll talk further.

Best regards,

Ron Davison
555-123-1234
ron@example.com
www.example.com

Keep it short and to the point, but it is extremely important that you include some uniquely memorable detail about your talk with Jane. This will help separate your email out from all the other emails Jane will receive. Also, by sending the email now you can confirm that you've correctly captured Jane's contact information—if the email bounces, make sure you've still got Jane's business card, and if you've lost it, you have time to hot-foot it back to Jane's booth and make sure you have the correct information!

Set a calendar reminder for a week's time to call Jane if you haven't heard from her by then.

PLANNING IT OUT

The journey home from the trade show is a great opportunity to think. When you're at a trade show it's very easy to get caught up in the excitement, so it's good to take this time to consider what you've learned while everything is fresh in your mind.

Ask yourself:

- Are you still in love with the product?
- Do you still think you can work well with Jane?

If you're still feeling great about moving forward, then it's time to hash out what you want to achieve, and what you can commit to. An exclusivity agreement has to work for both parties. You've got to make certain that you're not overextending yourself. Can you devote the time this is going to take, and can you afford the financial commitments? Thinking about all of this, take the time to plan out what you're going to ask for when you next talk to Jane.

ONE, SOME OR ALL SKUS?

How many different SKUs does Jane carry? How many different product lines? Assuming that Jane has several product lines, do you like them all, and if so, do you want to carry all of them? Do you like some SKUs in a particular product line, and some of another? It's perfectly acceptable to start with selling less than the entire product line of a vendor.

Here are some options you discuss:

- Exclusive on one SKU in one product line
- Exclusive on some SKUs in one product line
- Exclusive on all SKUs in one product line
- Exclusive on some SKUs in some product lines
- Exclusive on all SKUs in all product lines (everything the vendor sells)

TRIAL BASIS OR PERMANENT?

You might think that a permanent agreement would be the ultimate achievement at this point. Provided that Jane doesn't push for any penalties from you if you don't commit to buy a certain quantity, or decide that you no longer want to sell her products, this could indeed be the case, and in your best interests. However, if Jane wants you to commit to dollar or number requirements that you are not certain that you can meet, it might be best to commit to a one year agreement, with an option to renew the agreement if both parties agree.

USA OR WORLDWIDE?

Again, it might seem like a crowning achievement to scoop the worldwide rights, but at what cost? What are you committing to? If you are pushing for a worldwide exclusive, you need to be certain that you can uphold your end of the bargain.

Do you already have accounts open on worldwide platforms, like Amazon.ca or Amazon.co.uk? Do you have experience selling on these platforms? If not, are you willing to learn, and learn quickly?

OTHER CONSIDERATIONS

- Price: what will you pay for the products? Will you get a better price point if you have an exclusive?
- Marketing: who will undertake what? Will the vendor help with advertising costs? Will they market the product on their own, driving traffic to Amazon?
- Photos: who is responsible for product photography? Will the vendor be able to supply Amazon-compliant photos? If they can't will they help with the cost of photographing the products?
- Shipping: who is responsible for shipping costs?

These are just a few things that a contract can cover. You can ask for anything; the final contract will contain the terms you and the vendor both agree to.

Now, before you begin the negotiation write down at least three negotiation plans:

- A "best case" deal where you get exactly what you want
- A deal that you are satisfied with, but contains some compromises
- The minimum deal you are willing to accept – where anything less would literally be a "deal breaker"

Make sure your three plans outline what you want, what you will accept, and what you can commit to. Having a plan will mean that when you next talk to Jane, you will be more relaxed and able to make better decisions, because you're not going to have to think on the fly.

THE NEGOTIATION

Three days after the trade show, you get a phone call from Jane. She admits that she's exhausted after the show, and the prospect of partnering with someone to take some of the weight off her shoulders is now very appealing! It sounds like she's agreeable to an exclusivity agreement.

Now is the time to discuss the details. Because Jane called you, ask her what she proposes. Pay careful attention, and take notes as she talks. Ask clarifying questions to make sure you understand fully.

If she doesn't have a proposal, you can then make your own "Best Case" proposal.

During the negotiations, you're going to have to continuously test for reaction and make dynamic judgment calls. As soon as you sense that the vendor could be becoming uncomfortable, is having doubts, or is reluctant, then it's time to back off. Better to secure less of an exclusive than you wanted and have the opportunity to prove yourself to the vendor, than push for too much and lose it all. Be prepared to make compromises, but don't agree to anything less than your "minimum deal."

THE CONTRACT

Now that you and Jane have reached an agreement, where do you go from here? The next step is to have a contract drawn up by an attorney. You (or Jane) may question why you need a formal contract. The honest answer is that you don't, if you are both 100% sure as to what you are both agreeing to, and you are certain that the other person will abide by your agreement.

But since you and Jane have just met, and have no experience working together, how can you be certain of that? You probably both have the best of intentions, but it's better to have a professional listen to what you are both agreeing to, and distill it to something that is legally enforceable. Remember, a contract is not a guarantee that someone will abide by what they're agreeing to, rather, it sets out mutually agreed upon expectations, and the consequences for not meeting those expectations. As my attorney told me, a contract is just a "ticket to court," where you then have to prove that the other party broke the agreement.

Entering into a contract is not to be taken lightly, so make absolutely sure that you agree to everything it states prior to signing. A contract can always be modified later with the agreement of both parties, but that will most likely incur additional costs, so get everything locked down at the beginning.

Get two copies of the contract printed and signed – one for each of you. You really need an original signature, sometimes referred to as a "wet" signature, on all copies of the contract, so you'll have to send the documents back and forth. Sign both copies, send them to your vendor, and instruct them to sign both, keep one for their records, and send one back for you. Keep the original contract in a very safe place, such as a fireproof safe or a safe deposit box at your local bank.

Finally, once the deal is done, consider sending your vendor a small gift and a note saying how much you are looking forward to working with them. There are several Internet companies that provide the perfect small gifts for a very reasonable cost. I can't tell you how much goodwill this gesture will generate; it's a rare person who is thoughtful in this manner and it will make a big impression. It might mean that the vendor cuts you an even better deal in the future, or thinks of you first when other opportunities present themselves.

THE WORK BEGINS

Congratulations, you now have your first exclusive! Hopefully, it's the first of many.

CHAPTER 7 HOMEWORK

- Review the product lines you carry with an eye towards exclusives
- Research attorneys and exclusivity contracts

CHAPTER 7 RESOURCES

Business Card Reader Pro
- http://bit.ly/11wfMrK

Clifford Ennico (attorney for exclusive contracts)
- crennico@gmail.com

QR Stuff
- http://www.qrstuff.com

WORKING WITH SALES REPS

Sales reps are individuals who present and sell products to retailers. One company may employ them or they may represent several different companies. If they represent several companies, the product lines they represent will usually complement each other. They may work out of a wholesaler's office or warehouse, or they may work out of their own office. You'll also find sales reps that work from home.

Historically, there are two kinds of sales reps, but with the advent of the Internet, the lines between the two are blurring. Inside reps interact with their customers over the phone or on the Internet, while outside reps visit their customers face-to-face.

Sales reps can be a vital part of your business, if you know how to use reps to your advantage. In our eCommerce world, it's easy to think that the only way we can place our wholesale orders is directly online and over the phone with the wholesaler. While this is true, you miss a vital piece of the wholesale puzzle when you fail to work with the sales rep for the product line.

In most cases, sales reps get paid a commission for all orders placed in your territory, whether you utilize them or not. If you don't take advantage of what they have to offer you are leaving money on the table. You may not save real dollars working with the rep but you will be gaining valuable knowledge about the product line, upcoming products, closeouts, and more. And in this business, that kind of knowledge is money.

While we don't believe everything the sales rep says is in our best interest, we do believe they bring a wealth of knowledge to the game. Also, most sales reps that see you in person, or hear your voice over the phone on a regular basis, do not want an unhappy client. They want your product to sell-through as much as you do, and will do what they can to help you.

If they are an honest and frank sales rep, you will make money by taking time to talk with them on a regular basis. Listening to a rep can be tough for those of us who are self-motivated, independent thinkers. It can be hard to ask for help, even from a sales rep, but we really recommend you use the rep to your advantage.

Some of the things you can expect from a sales rep:

- You'll hear about deals, sales and specials. You'll find out about products that are being discontinued at a markdown price. This kind of knowledge can be invaluable when it comes knowing that a product will soon be hard to find.

- You'll learn if the brand is highly protected. You'll find out if they have a team in their company that polices MAP. We both love brands that police MAP violations.

- You'll find out if they allow Amazon onto a line immediately or if they have an agreement that newer products are available only to other resellers, not to Amazon. This will protect you from Amazon coming in and taking over a line.

- You will learn the inner workings of a company and how they work with different platforms and different resellers.

- You'll find out how the line is performing overall. A good sales rep will tell you when one of their lines has been a flop.

- You'll learn which product lines are having an anniversary year and what the company plans to do to celebrate. Companies put their marketing efforts into overdrive during an anniversary year. This is a huge piece of knowledge because the marketing efforts can spread across many wholesale lines and categories. There can also be special anniversary products ... like the Dorothy doll created for the Wizard of Oz 75th anniversary. The doll has an MSRP of $25 but was selling for close to $100 by resellers on Amazon.

A final word of caution: be careful not to waste the sales rep's time. After all, we are all in the industry where time is money and while you may find their information valuable, if you don't place an order, they probably won't continue to be as enthusiastic in sharing that valuable information with you. And I think we can all agree that that is fair!

CHAPTER 8 HOMEWORK

- Check with your current wholesale accounts and find out who your sales rep is
- Organize the information about your reps! They are of no value to you if you cannot find them. Use Google Docs, a contact management program, or Evernote

CHAPTER 8 RESOURCES

Evernote
- http://www.evernote.com

Google Docs
- http://www.docs.google.com

BRINGING PRODUCTS
TO MARKET

To be successful we both feel you must be willing to introduce products to the Amazon marketplace. This is scary proposition for new sellers and sometimes even seasoned ones feel some trepidation, but being the first to market with a product is a huge opportunity. Not only will you capture all the sales for the product (at least in the beginning), successful launches to Amazon will set you apart from the average Amazon seller, something wholesalers look for when choosing who they want to work with.

Charlene and Darla have both had a lot of success bringing products to the Amazon marketplace. They both follow very similar paths when looking for products and dealing with the wholesalers of those products.

First, you must know your niche. That means you must know the hot products and the hot brands. You must also know trends in the niche. Subscribe to trade publications in the niche, read blogs, and talk to wholesalers. Pinterest and

Instagram can also help you spot trends in a niche. We also suggest you check out sites like Trendhunter and Trendwatching for more information about trends and how to discover them and use the information to your advantage.

Know your strengths and your weakness. Do you dislike creating product listings? Do you like putting together bundles? If you hate making new listings, don't let that stop you from bringing products to market. You can always hire someone to write the listings for you.

If you like putting together bundles for Amazon, you have a huge advantage over other sellers. You need to leverage that advantage and constantly be thinking about putting together bundles that cannot be recreated easily by other sellers. As you develop your bundles for Amazon, remember Charlene's mantra: every item in the bundle must add value for the buyer. Anything less does you and the buyer both a disservice.

What successes have you had with current products on Amazon? Knowing what has done well for you in the past gives you insight into which products might do well for you in the future. Have you had success with wine-related products? Seek out vendors of new products in the wine niche. And conversely, if you have found that a certain type of product has not been as successful as you would like, think twice about bring new products of that type to Amazon, unless your gut tells you that the product is different and unique enough to buck the trend.

What successes have you witnessed on Amazon but couldn't get your hands on the products from a wholesaler? For example, OXO products are very difficult to obtain from wholesale sources, but the success of their product line (soft handles, easy-to-read measurements, etc.) might lead you to look at similar products in other lines. An aging baby boomer population might mean that the market for these types of products will grow.

Look for unique items. Why is the product you are bringing to market different than all the others out there? Or is it just a difference in packaging, or a slight size difference?

Look for a hole in the market. Does a particular brand or product often go out of stock? Perhaps you can find something similar in another line that can fill in the hole when the other product is out of stock; if it is a good product momentum can grow and sales can continue to happen whether the original product is in stock or not.

Perhaps there is a color or a fragrance not represented on Amazon in the present popular line. Can you get the missing item? Or can you find that missing piece in a different line? Say you found that a line of kitchen canisters sells really well, but there are no yellow canisters in that line. Yellow is a popular kitchen accent color. Can you find yellow canisters in another line?

Are there already several brands that are a similar product? If this is the case, you probably need to steer clear unless you are confident in that brand. This is where knowing your niche is really important.

Watch the category size carefully. A small Amazon category like Pets requires more product knowledge than a large category like Toys. There is less room for error in a small category, but a small category is easier to learn and master than an enormous category.

Remember, Amazon's gated categories are still gated, even if you bring a product to market. So if you are intent on bringing products to Amazon in a certain category, make sure you are eligible to sell in that category. If you aren't, do the steps to get approved before you spend time on a lot of research and money on products.

Never overestimate the taste of the American public ... we have both found that tacky sells. Why else would millions of Chia Pets and Big Mouth Billy Bass products have sold? No matter what your personal taste, you have to get real with yourself. Just because you like it doesn't mean thousands of other people will. If you're lucky a few hundred will like it, if you're not, well, good thing you like it, because you might be living with them for a while. Conversely, just because you think it is the worst thing you have ever seen doesn't mean hundreds or thousands or millions of other people won't buy it. It's hard to keep personal taste out of the mix, but you really have to be objective when looking for new products.

Once you have determined new products you want to bring to Amazon, and have done the groundwork with the manufacturer, we have a few more hints for you to make the process as easy and as profitable as possible.

Ask the manufacturer if they will provide high-resolution images of the products on a white background. If they don't have the images, they might be willing to take them for you. Make sure you get large (we suggest over 1500 pixels on the longest side but 1001 pixels on the longest side will work as well) images on a white background that reads 255,255,255 on the RGB scale. If you can't get images with the pure white background, and don't want to spend the time learning to remove the background yourself, you can use a service like Remove the Background to do it for you.

Besides product selection, we both agree that keywords are the single biggest factor in determining whether a product launch on Amazon will be successful or not. In a nutshell, keywords are words used in product title, descriptions, bullet points, and in the keyword field in the Amazon listing form.

When crafting new product listings, we believe that bullet points are more important than the product description to the Amazon shopper. This is because people prefer to skim highlights instead of reading paragraphs, and bullet points show "above the fold" so people don't have to scroll to read them. So make sure your bullet points are relevant and compelling and be sure to use keywords where appropriate.

A great description, one that describes the product and provides features and benefits, will also help sell your product. Especially with higher-priced products, a well-written, accurate description can help people make the decision to buy the product. And a good product description, optimized to rank highly in Google search, will help shoppers find your product on Google.

As you can imagine, there is an art and a craft to selecting keywords and writing good product listings. Besides knowing Amazon's policies and styles as they relate to listings, you also need to know where to find good keywords for your product, and how to write sales copy that will convince people to buy your product.

And this is where Karon Thackston's book *Amazon Advantage: Product Listing Strategies to Boost Your Sales* comes in. Karen has written an e-book that covers the art of writing Amazon product listings in depth. With information about keywords, product positioning, buyer psychology, and more, her book will take the mystery out of writing Amazon product listings. Karon also includes separate worksheets so you can have one worksheet for each product listing and save them for future reference.

You now have all the pieces you need to bring new products to the Amazon marketplace. Do your research and study the market and you will be able to successfully bring new products to Amazon and capitalize on those sales.

CHAPTER 9 HOMEWORK

- Find three products that are not currently on Amazon to research
- Research sales of related products and trends and identify one product to bring to Amazon
- Do the deal ... obtain the product, write the listing and send to Amazon

CHAPTER 9 RESOURCES

Amazon Image Requirements
- http://amzn.to/1vB5Fvw

Remove the Background
- http://www.removethebackground.com

Trendhunter
- http://www.trendhunter.com

Trendwatching
- http://trendwatching.com

MANAGING THE DETAILS

There is no getting around the fact that wholesale sourcing creates paperwork. There are catalogs, invoices, packing slips, price sheets and more to keep track of. You have to manage pending orders, shipments, and payments. Keeping track of all this can be a daunting task. Fortunately, if you develop a system and use that system religiously, you'll save yourself time and stress when it comes to finding that business card for a sales rep or the price sheet from the line you want to order.

SUPPLIERS

We suggest you have a separate folder (meaning folder on your computer and a physical folder as well) for each of your suppliers. In these folders, put your catalogs, price sheets, business cards, and any other information that relates to that company. Both Charlene and Darla like hard copies of catalogs. They both find it easier to thumb through a physical catalog than click through a PDF catalog.

It may happen that you have a wholesale account that goes dormant. It could be because you had to open the account in order to find out pricing, or the product didn't measure up to your standards. Dormant account files can be filed in an archive area of your filing cabinet. Active accounts should be kept in an easily accessible area.

Darla uses Google Docs to keep track of her wholesale supply chain. She stores price sheets and contact information there, along with user names, passwords and whether there is a MAP pricing contract in place. She also keeps contact information about her sales reps in Google Docs.

Charlene uses a combination of Evernote and Contacts (a Mac address book built into OS X) to keep track of all her wholesale information. PDFs of catalogs, price lists, and other details are stored in Evernote, and contact info for companies and sales reps is stored in Contacts. Both of these programs sync across both her mobile and desktop devices so the information is available no matter what piece of technology she is using at the time.

ORDERS

Darla uses a Google Docs spreadsheet to keep track of her orders. She has a spreadsheet for each order. Everyone on her team has access to the spreadsheets, so they can work as a team toward the end goal, which is getting product out the door.

Charlene uses Evernote to keep copies of pending orders. When an order is placed online and the confirmation screen appears, she uses the Evernote Web Clipper to put a copy of the order into her Pending Orders notebook.

When an order arrives, both Charlene and Darla pull out the order sheets to check it against the packing list and confirm that all the ordered items were received. They both check off each item as they unpack the box, examining items for damage as they are unpacked. When they have verified that the order is complete, they file the invoice and packing slip.

SKUS

Every business has its own method for recording and tracking SKUS. Darla and Charlene have different methods of assigning SKUs. Darla's SKUs contain the initials of the wholesaler, the item number, and the cost.

Currently, Charlene's SKUs contain only the item number as assigned by the wholesaler, and she wishes she had started using initials of the wholesaler at the beginning of each SKU to make sorting by wholesaler and reordering products easier and more efficient.

CHAPTER 10 HOMEWORK

- Set up a system for organizing paperwork from your wholesalers
- Earmark a place for catalogs, price sheets and other vendor information

CHAPTER 10 RESOURCES

Evernote
- http://www.evernote.com

Google Docs
- http://www.docs.google.com

EVALUATING PRODUCTS

Researching the products you are interested in sourcing involves two major areas: price research and everything else. We like to look at research this way because if the price doesn't work for you and your business, nothing else matters. But before you get into doing deep research into prices, there are a few things you need to ask yourself about the products you are considering.

First, look on Amazon to see what the marketplace for that wholesale line looks like in general. With the Amazon search page open in your browser, ask yourself the following questions:

- Is Amazon selling their line?
- What is the ASP (average sales price) for the top 10 products in the line?
- Are any of the products add-ons?
- What are the ranks for their top 10 products?
- Are most of the products in the top 10 in gated categories? Are you approved to sell in those categories?

- Do you recognize any of the third party sellers? (If you are brand new the answer is probably no). Why is that important? When you know who the other sellers are, and have followed them long enough you know if they'll follow MAP or undercut prices.
- How many sellers are on the listings? How many of those are FBA sellers?
- Are you approved to sell in the category on Amazon?
- Is there a possibility the item is classified as HazMat? If it is, and you are not approved by Amazon to send in HazMat items, are you willing to merchant fulfill the product?

Over the years we have learned that there are other sticking points when we are looking at products to source. Here are some of them:

- Halloween items will often fall under clothing and accessories, so be careful. Halloween products will sometimes start out in toys and games and get moved to clothing, as Halloween gets closer.
- Small niche categories (like Baby) may be less viable than the big categories, like Home and Garden.
- A seller who doesn't have approval to sell the product in a gated category usually puts products in the Everything Else category. Products in EE are severely hampered in search results ... so have it moved to the proper category.

CHAPTER 11 HOMEWORK

- Evaluate product lines from three wholesalers

OUTSOURCING THE WORK

Your business is growing, and there aren't enough hours in the day to get everything done. If you want to continue growing, you can hire employees or use third party services to buy more time.

THIRD PARTY PREP SERVICES

There are many companies that will help you with your Amazon business by doing the product processing for you, and it seems like a new one pops up every week. To use a service like these, you have your wholesaler ship the items to the service company and they will label, bag, and ship your items to the appropriate Amazon warehouses. But before you jump in and hire one of these companies to do the processing for you, you need to do some homework.

Not all services are created equal. We both have strong feelings about things that are non-negotiable when you look for a processing service, and the first is that a non-disclosure and non-compete agreements are musts. If the service won't sign these agreements, don't get involved with them. You are giving the service access to the names of your wholesalers and the products you sell. Without these agreements, how can you be sure the company won't contact the wholesalers and start sourcing the products? You can't be sure. So get those agreements signed before you send products to the service.

Hiring a service doesn't do away with all of the work involved in processing inventory. You still need to enter the products into your inventory on Amazon and create labels and shipments, and then send PDFs to the service. What you won't have to do is label and bag the products, repack them, and get them to UPS. That's what the service will do for you.

A service that is located close to the majority of your wholesalers will be more cost effective than one located across the country, so keep location in mind when researching services. Ask about turn around time ... how fast do they process shipments, and do they have a guarantee that your orders will be processed within a certain period of time?

Find out how they handle items that are damaged in shipping. Do they alert you to the damaged products? Do they send images so you can decide how to handle them? Or do they just blindly process without regard to the condition of the item?

How do they handle shortages from the wholesaler? Do they contact you immediately upon discovery? Or do they ship the order to Amazon short?

What happens when items are damaged in shipment from the service to Amazon? Do they take responsibility? Do they reimburse you? Or do they leave you to the mercy of Amazon to try to get reimbursed?

We both believe that if something can go wrong in the process, it will. So make sure that you and the service are clear in how errors are handled, and who takes responsibility for those errors. We are all human, and mistakes happen, but the true value of the service will be revealed when you find out how they handle those problems.

You are putting a big part of your business in someone else's hands, and you must do your due diligence before you release control of your inventory to someone else. In the end, it is your seller account and your metrics that will suffer if the prep service doesn't do its job properly.

These services can be costly, and prices vary widely, so shop around. Some services have monthly minimums, some don't. Some services have sliding price scales, meaning the more items you send in, the lower the price you pay per item for processing. When running the numbers, make sure your margins can handle the costs that a prep service will add to your cost of goods. If you have more time than money, we suggest you process your orders yourself until the time/money balance tips in the other direction.

Amazon also has prep services that will label, bag and bubble wrap your products. You can find the link to details about their services and prices on the Resource page.

Pros to using a prep service:

- You don't have to physically handle the products.
- You don't need to purchase and store supplies like boxes and tape.
- Using a service can possibly free up time and energy.
- Nobody has to be home for your products to be received.
- Your UPS, Federal Express and USPS drivers won't hate you.

Cons to using a prep service:

- It can be costly; watch for monthly minimums.
- Nobody cares as much about your product as you do and may not inspect as carefully as you would.
- Items damaged in shipping may be overlooked.
- If you have not seen the product before, you may not have the UPC, picture or dimensions for listing.
- Slight variations in the product may not be caught by the service.
- Some services will not sign non-disclosure and non-compete agreements, leaving you open to direct competition.
- You will still need to enter inventory and create labels and shipments.
- A service located far away from your wholesalers and your warehouses may dramatically increase your shipping costs.

EMPLOYEES AND INDEPENDENT CONTRACTORS

As your business grows, the next logical step for many people is to hire help for repetitive tasks like labeling and bagging. Here are some things you should keep in mind when looking to hire someone to help you in your business.

Decide if you want to hire an employee or if you want to hire an independent contractor. There are pluses and minuses to each situation, and only you can determine which direction is best for your business. You have to think about things like payroll taxes, worker's compensation insurance, and dozens of other details. There are lots of comparisons of the two hiring methods online, including ones from the IRS and from Legal Zoom. You can find the link in the Resources section at the end of this chapter.

Whether you hire an independent contractor or an employee, there are general business procedures that relate to both, so for the sake of simplicity in this chapter, we will call them employees.

First and foremost, if you are selling on Amazon, never relinquish control of your seller account to an employee. You can assign user permissions through Amazon to grant employees access to the parts of your account they need to do the job, but never relinquish access to your entire account.

Carefully oversee the work of a new employee for the first month and spot check his work at random times throughout the year. Make sure the spot checks are random and you check different areas of his work each time. Darla likes the phrase "Inspect what you expect." Don't get complacent. It is your responsibility to make sure the work is being done properly.

Should you pay your employees by the hour or by the piece? Both are viable options. Hiring by the hour requires that you motivate employees on a regular basis to keep up productivity. Setting basic expectations for the number of items to be processed per hour lets employees know if they are meeting your standards and whether they need to speed up their work.

Hiring by the piece can also work, but remember, having someone race against the clock isn't always efficient or productive, or accurate. If you chose to pay by the piece, set clear expectations as they relate to the job, and check on a regular basis that the work is being done carefully and accurately. Think about instituting a maximum number of pieces per hour to be processed so employees remain as error-free as possible.

Set up incentives so each team member feels valued. Whether this is a bonus, paid time off, or a lunch out, make sure you have something in place to show employees that you appreciate their work.

Meet with your employees on a regular basis to review their work and your expectations. In this meeting, ask about their impressions of the job and what they think can be done to make their work more accurate and more efficient. Never underestimate employee suggestions; they may have thought of a way of doing things that hadn't crossed your mind. If they come up with a suggestion that truly improves your business, a reward of some kind is certainly in order.

If the employee will need a computer to do his job, will you provide it, or will he? If you provide a computer, it must be a secondary computer because you will still need yours to do your job ... whether it be sourcing, paying bills, or answering e-mails. If you have to give up your computer for an employee to use to get his job done, you are not going to be productive; you will end up frustrated and impatient.

Having properly working equipment is absolutely vital. Don't expect employees to know how to fix your scale, or where to order replacement wires for your impulse sealer. Have the supplies and equipment in place that they need to do their jobs. Nothing is worse than having to pay an employee who can't work because you ran out of poly bags.

If you are an introvert it can be a challenge to have someone else around while you work. While it can be fun if you love to interact with people, for some it can be difficult. Know your personality type and what makes you uncomfortable. If you really want an employee to help, set out guidelines when you hire ... whether chitchat is OK, or if you prefer silence in the workplace. You also need to set expectations for their behavior while on the clock. Will you allow texting, or personal phone calls? Can they surf the web? How long are breaks? Make sure you have expectations clearly spelled out so your employee knows what is expected of him.

If you have an employee you may find that there may be times when he isn't as busy as you would like. Don't get caught up in the cycle of buying sub-par products just to keep your employee busy. If they run out of work to do, you can have him do jobs that often get pushed to the back burner in the rush to get products out the door. They can do inventory of boxes, bags, labels and other supplies, or organize your storage space, or 1001 other things that always need doing.

If you know you are coming up on a period where you won't need the employee for the hours per week that you agreed to, discuss it with him as soon as you know. He is counting on the hours you promised and if you can't offer them, he may need to look for temporary work elsewhere until you can offer the hours he needs.

Do your due diligence when hiring any employee. Remember, you are opening your life and your livelihood to this employee. In many cases, you'll be working out of your home so you'll be opening your home as well. If you are a woman, take extra care if you are hiring a male employee. Your personal safety is more important than having an employee to lift boxes.

Run a background check on anyone you are considering hiring. An online background check costs about $30. Be sure you ask for references on your employment application, and don't stop there. Don't just check the references, talk to people in your community about their experiences with the prospective employee.

Listen to your gut feeling. If something doesn't seem right to you, pay attention. Instinct can go a long way in ensuring you hire the right person.

If all of this seems too much, you can hire an agency to handle all of the detail work for you. Employment agencies can do the background checks, check references, and handle employee payment and payroll taxes.

CHAPTER 12 HOMEWORK

- Decide what jobs you could easily outsource
- Draw up basic job descriptions for those jobs

CHAPTER 12 RESOURCES

Amazon Prep Service
- http://www.amazon.com/gp/help/customer/display.html/?nodeId=201131680

Legal Zoom
- https://www.legalzoom.com/articles/employee-vs-independent-contractor-differences-you-need-to-know

GLOSSARY

Asset: property owned by a person or company, regarded as having value and available to meet debts and other commitments. An asset might be cash in the bank, inventory, or shipping supplies.

Balance Sheet: a statement that shows the financial condition of a company at a specific moment in time. A balance sheet lists the amount of money and property that the company owns and the amount of money it owes.

Bill of Lading (sometimes abbreviated as B/L or BoL): is a document issued by a carrier which details a shipment of merchandise and gives title of that shipment to a specified party. BoLs are especially important for international shipments.

Brand: a category of products that are all made by a particular company and all have a particular name. Examples include Revlon, Tupperware, and Chanel.

Broker: an individual or company that arranges transactions between a buyer and seller. A broker does not carry inventory; instead they act as a middleman between buyer and seller. They are usually paid a commission when the deal is completed.

Case Pack: the number of selling units in a shipping case. A case pack may or may not be the minimum amount a wholesaler will sell to you.

Cash and Carry: a system of wholesale trading whereby goods are paid for in full at the time of purchase and taken away by the purchaser. You'll find cash and carry at some trade shows and merchandise marts.

COD (Cash On Delivery): the system of paying for goods when they are delivered. In some cases, wholesalers will ask new buyers to purchase products COD, This means you will pay whoever delivers the goods (UPS, etc.) for the merchandise at the time of delivery. This has become less common with the explosion of credit card acceptance by wholesalers.

Credit References: the name of an individual, or the name of a business that can provide details about your past track record with credit.

Distributor: often used interchangeably with the term "wholesaler." A distributor may supply products from just one manufacturer, or can supply products from several different manufacturers.

Drop Ship: a business model and an inventory management technique in which the retailer does not keep goods in stock, but instead transfers customer orders and shipment details to either the manufacturer or a wholesaler, who then ships the goods directly to the customer.

FEIN (Federal Employer Identification Number): the nine-digit number that the IRS assigns to organizations. The IRS uses the number to identify taxpayers. We like to call it the Social Security number for your business. You do not need to have employees to have an FEIN.

FOB (Free On Board): responsibility for freight costs is determined by the suffix "Origin" or "Destination" after "FOB" in the seller's terms. "FOB Origin" indicates that the sale is considered complete at the seller's shipping dock, and the company buying the goods is responsible for freight costs. "FOB Destination" means the sale is complete at the buyer's doorstep and the seller is responsible for freight costs.

Forklift: a vehicle with a pronged device in front for lifting and carrying heavy loads such as pallets.

Gift Shop: a store primarily selling gifts and souvenirs relating to a particular topic or theme. Gift shops are common in malls and tourist areas.

Gift Show: a show, whether permanent or temporary, that caters to buyers of products typically carried in gift shops. Stores that find products at gift shows include resort and hotel gift shops, hospital gift shops, home furnishing stores, and garden centers.

Gross: twelve dozen, or 144 units. Some wholesalers will sell items by the gross.

Gross Sales: the grand total of all sale transactions reported in a period, without any deductions such as cost of inventory.

Income Statement: a financial statement that summarizes the revenues, costs and expenses incurred during a specific period of time, usually a fiscal quarter or year.

Inner Case or Inner Pack: an additional level of multi-unit packaging within a case or carton. As an example, you may have a case that contains 100 units of an item, but within that case you have 10 smaller boxes that each contain 10 units. These smaller packages are called inner cases or inner packs.

Invoice: a commercial document issued by a seller to a buyer. An invoice will typically contain the word "Invoice," the date, the name and address of both the buyer and seller, a purchase order or sales order number, the quantity, description and unit price for the products purchased, payment terms, and delivery or shipment date.

Keystone Pricing (keystoning): a pricing method where merchandise is priced for resale at double the wholesale price.

Letter of Credit: a letter issued by a bank to another bank (typically in a different country) to serve as a guarantee for payments made to a specified person under specified conditions. Letters of Credit are most commonly used for large purchases from companies in another country. A company may require a LoC to protect them while they manufacture your 10,000 units of their product.

Liability: an obligation of a person or business arising from past transactions or events. A liability could be an outstanding invoice from a supplier, a phone bill, or the balance on a credit card.

Lift Gate: a device at the rear of a vehicle that can be mechanically raised during loading and unloading of cargo. A truck with a lift gate is needed to unload pallets if you do not have a loading dock.

Liquidation: the process by which a company is brought to an end, and the assets and property of the company are redistributed. The term is also used when a company wants to divest itself of some of its assets. For instance, a retail chain wants to close some of their stores. They will sell the inventory to a company that specializes in store liquidation. These companies may sell the remaining inventory in the retail location or may move it to a warehouse or other storefront and sell it there.

Loading Dock: a raised platform where trucks or trains can be loaded or unloaded.

Line (or Product Line): several related products that are for sale individually. A product line like Pantene may contain products like shampoo, conditioner and hairspray, while another line like Sharpie will contain markers in a variety of sizes and colors.

Line Sheet: also called wholesale sales sheet, a line sheet is used by a manufacturer to provide information about their products. It may include the name, the UPC, the SKU, the wholesale price, and the suggested retail price.

MAP (Minimum Advertised Price): an agreement between suppliers and retailers stipulating the lowest price at which an item is allowed to be advertised. MAP agreements are valuable tools for both the manufacturer and retailer, as they can help prevent the "race to the bottom" and can help reinforce the brand value.

Mart or Market: a permanent location where manufacturers and wholesalers are set up in showrooms to display their products to buyers. In addition to the permanent showrooms, marts and markets may also have temporary exhibitors ("temporaries") that are set up for a short, specific period of time.

Mixed SKUs: a variety of SKUs shipped in one box (see SKU).

MOQ (Minimum Order Quantity): the smallest amount a manufacturer or wholesaler will allow you to order. A MOQ can be a dollar amount (for example, $250), or a specified number of items (for example, 50 units).

MSRP: The manufacturer's suggested retail price of a product is the price which the manufacturer recommends the retailer sell the product. The intention is to help to standardize prices among locations.

Net: the amount remaining after all deductions have been made.

Net of Discount: some wholesalers will use this terminology when noting their minimum orders. $500 net of discount means that your order must total $500 after the wholesale and any other discounts are applied.

Opening Order: the first order placed with a wholesaler. Most wholesalers will have a minimum requirement for an opening order. That minimum can be a dollar minimum or a quantity minimum.

Outsourcing: the contracting out of a business process to a third party. For example, you can outsource your bookkeeping, your packing and shipping, or your inventory reconciliation.

Pallet: a flat structure that supports goods in a stable fashion while being lifted by a forklift, pallet jack, or other device. Goods placed on a pallet are often secured with strapping or stretch wrap. Most pallets are wooden, but pallets can also be made of plastic or metal.

Pallet Jack: also known as a pallet truck, pallet pump, pump truck, or jigger, a pallet jack is a tool used to lift and move pallets. It doesn't raise them enough to get them in a truck (you need a forklift for that) but the pallet jack allows for easy movement of pallets within a warehouse, or onto a truck if you have a loading dock.

Profit: the financial benefit that is realized when the amount of revenue gained from a business activity (such as selling on Amazon or eBay) exceeds the expenses, costs and taxes needed to sustain the activity.

Profit Margin: the amount by which revenue from sales exceeds costs.

Reorder: the second and subsequent orders to a manufacturer or wholesaler. Typically, reorder requirements (whether a dollar amount or quantity) are smaller than the initial or opening order. For example, the opening order requirement may be $300 but reorders are $150. In actuality, if you have found a good product or products, your reorders will be larger than your opening order.

Resale Number: also known as Sales Tax Certificate, Resale Certificate or Tax Exempt Certificate, resale numbers are issued by each state, and are used when purchasing items for resale. Most wholesalers require that you provide them with your resale number when you apply to open an account. States that do not have sales tax will provide business certificates that can be used in the same manner. For example, Oregon calls their certificate a Business Registry Resale Certificate.

Reseller: a company or individual that purchases goods or services with the intention of reselling them rather than consuming or using them.

Retail: the sale of goods to the public in relatively small quantities for use or consumption rather than for resale.

RMA (Return Merchandise Authorization): an RMA is a part of the process of returning a product to a wholesaler. You must contact the wholesaler to obtain authorization to return the product. The resulting RMA number must be displayed on and included in the returned product's packaging.

ROI (Return on investment): a measure of profit. In simple terms, the ROI formula is

$$ROI = (return - cost)/cost \times 100$$

You can also calculate ROI over specified periods of time, such as monthly or yearly. For more detailed calculations, there are apps like ROI Calculator to help you with the calculations. See link on Resource page.

Sales Rep (Sales Representative): a person or organization designated by a company to solicit business on its behalf in a specified territory.

SEO (Search Engine Optimization): the process of increasing the visibility of a website or a web page in a search engine's natural, unpaid search results. SEO considers how search engines work, what people search for, the actual search terms or keywords typed into search engines, and which search engines are preferred by their targeted audience.

SKU (Stock Keeping Unit): an identification code that is assigned to a distinct item, consisting of numbers and/or letters. For example, a red T-shirt and a blue T-shirt would have different SKUs because they are not identical items.

Temporaries: temporary exhibitors that are set up for a short, specific period of time at places like America's Mart and Dallas Market Center.

Terms: the agreement as to how an order is to be paid for. Net 10, Net 15, Net 30 and Net 60 are forms of credit which specify that the total outstanding amount on the invoice is expected to be paid in full and received by the seller within 10, 15, 30 or 60 days after the goods are shipped.

Net 30 or Net 60 terms are often coupled with a credit for early payment, such as 2/10 Net 30, which means you receive a 2% discount if you pay in full within 10 days, and if you choose not to pay in 10 days, the entire invoice is due in 30 days.

Trade References: the name of a business or supplier in your field. Many wholesalers want trade references to prove that you are a legitimate business.

Trade Show: an exhibition for companies in a specific industry to showcase and demonstrate their new products and services. Generally trade shows are not open to the public and can only be attended by company buyers and members of the press. Company buyers can place orders for products at a trade show.

UPC (Universal Product Code): a barcode that is widely used for tracking inventory.

Wholesale: the selling of goods in large quantities to be retailed by others.

BUSINESS REGISTRATION

ALABAMA
- http://www.sos.state.al.us/downloads/corpForms.aspx

ALASKA
- http://commerce.alaska.gov/dnn/ded/FIN/BusinessPla nningAssistance.aspx

ARIZONA
- http://www.azcc.gov/Divisions/Corporations/where-do-i-start.asp
- http://www.azdor.gov/Business/LicensingGuide.aspx

ARKANSAS
- http://www.dfa.arkansas.gov/offices/policyAndLegal/Documents/starting_a-new_business.pdf
- https://atap.arkansas.gov/_/#2

CALIFORNIA
- http://www.sos.ca.gov/business/be/forms.htm

COLORADO

- http://www.colorado.gov/cs/Satellite/Revenue/REVX/1251624713753

CONNECTICUT

- http://www.concord-sots.ct.gov/CONCORD/index.jsp?ctportalPNavCtr=|27196|#45040

DELAWARE

- https://onestop.delaware.gov/osbrlpublic/

FLORIDA

- http://dor.myflorida.com/dor/info_business.html
- http://dor.myflorida.com/dor/forms/current/gt300015.pdf

GEORGIA

- https://gtc.dor.ga.gov/_/#1

HAWAII

- http://cca.hawaii.gov/breg/
- https://hbe.ehawaii.gov/BizEx/home.eb
- http://files.hawaii.gov/tax/legal/taxfacts/tf97-03.pdf

IDAHO

- http://tax.idaho.gov/i-1159.cfm

ILLINOIS

- http://www.revenue.state.il.us/businesses/register.htm

INDIANA

- http://www.in.gov/ai/appfiles/sos-registration/landing.html

IOWA

- https://www.idr.iowa.gov/CBA/start.asp

KANSAS

- https://www.accesskansas.org/businesscenter/

KENTUCKY

- http://revenue.ky.gov/business/register.htm

LOUISIANA

- http://www.revenue.louisiana.gov/sections/business/intro.aspx

MAINE

- http://www.maine.gov/portal/business/starting.html

MARYLAND

- http://casy.maryland.gov/

MASSACHUSETTS

- http://www.mass.gov/portal/business/start-business/

MICHIGAN

- http://www.michigan.gov/business

MINNESOTA

- http://www.revenue.state.mn.us/businesses/Pages/Business-Registration.aspx

MISSISSIPPI

- http://www.sos.ms.gov/BusinessServices/Pages/default.aspx

MISSOURI

- http://dor.mo.gov/business/register/

MONTANA

- http://sos.mt.gov/business/Startup/index.asp

NEBRASKA

- http://www.revenue.nebraska.gov/business/bus_regist.html

NEVADA

- https://www.nvsilverflume.gov/home#start-your-business

NEW HAMPSHIRE

- http://www.nheconomy.com/business-services/starting-a-business-in-nh.aspx

NEW JERSEY

- http://www.state.nj.us/njbusiness/registration/

NEW MEXICO
- http://www.tax.newmexico.gov/Businesses/register-your-business.aspx

NEW YORK
- http://www.tax.ny.gov/bus/multi/register_license.htm

NORTH CAROLINA
- http://www.blnc.gov/start-your-business

NORTH DAKOTA
- http://www.nd.gov/businessreg

OHIO
- http://www.tax.ohio.gov/other/other_resources_for_businesses.aspx

OKLAHOMA
- http://www.tax.ok.gov/busregonline.html
- http://www.tax.ok.gov/forms/busregpk.pdf

OREGON
- http://sos.oregon.gov/business/pages/business-information-center.aspx

PENNSYLVANIA
- http://www.doreservices.state.pa.us/BusinessTax/PA100/FormatSelection.htm
- http://www.portal.state.pa.us/portal/server.pt/community/business_registration_forms/19096

RHODE ISLAND
- http://www.ri.gov/taxation/BAR/

SOUTH CAROLINA
- http://www.sos.sc.gov/forms/Business%20Opportunities/Registeration%20Form.pdf
- http://www.sos.sc.gov/forms/BusinessFilingDocumentRequestForm.pdf

SOUTH DAKOTA
- https://apps.sd.gov/applications/rv23cedar/main/main.aspx

TENNESSEE
- http://www.tn.gov/revenue/business/startingnewbus.shtml

TEXAS
- http://www.sos.state.tx.us/corp/forms_boc.shtml

UTAH
- http://osbr.utah.gov/

VERMONT
- http://www.state.vt.us/tax/businessstarting.shtml

VIRGINIA
- http://www.tax.virginia.gov/site.cfm?alias=RegBus

WASHINGTON
- http://dor.wa.gov/Content/DoingBusiness/RegisterMy Business/

WEST VIRGINIA
- https://www.business4wv.com/b4wvpublic/default.aspx

WISCONSIN
- http://www.revenue.wi.gov/NewBusiness.html

WYOMING
- http://soswy.state.wy.us/business/Default.aspx
- http://www.wyomingbusiness.org/program/business-permitting/2833
- https://doe.state.wy.us/wyereg/

SALES TAX REGISTRATION

ALABAMA
- http://revenue.alabama.gov/salestax/register.cfm
- https://myalabamataxes.alabama.gov/_/#1

ALASKA
- http://commerce.alaska.gov/dnn/dcra/OfficeoftheState Assessor/AlaskaSalesTaxInformation.aspx

ARIZONA
- http://www.azdor.gov/Business/TransactionPrivilege Tax.aspx
- https://www.aztaxes.gov/default.aspx

ARKANSAS
- http://www.dfa.arkansas.gov/offices/exciseTax/salesa nduse/Pages/default.aspx
- https://atap.arkansas.gov/_/#3

CALIFORNIA
- http://www.boe.ca.gov/sutax/faqseller.htm

COLORADO

- http://www.colorado.gov/cs/Satellite/Revenue/REVX/1251608978938

CONNECTICUT

- http://www.ct.gov/drs/cwp/view.asp?a=1454&q=508078

DELAWARE

- http://revenue.delaware.gov/services/Business_Tax/Exemptions.shtml

FLORIDA

- http://dor.myflorida.com/dor/taxes/annual_resale_certificate_sut.html

GEORGIA

- https://etax.dor.ga.gov/SearchResults.aspx?q=Apply+for+sales+tax+certificate

HAWAII

- http://tax.hawaii.gov/forms/a1_b2_1geuse/

IDAHO

- http://tax.idaho.gov/i-1033.cfm

ILLINOIS

- http://www.revenue.state.il.us/businesses/CRTinfo.htm

INDIANA
- http://www.in.gov/dor/3504.htm

IOWA
- http://www.iowa.gov/tax/business/temp.html

KANSAS
- http://www.ksrevenue.org/forms-btsales.html

KENTUCKY
- http://revenue.ky.gov/forms/cursalefrm.htm

LOUISIANA
- http://www.revenue.louisiana.gov/sections/business/resalecertificate.aspx

MAINE
- http://www.maine.gov/revenue/salesuse/salestax/salestax.html

MARYLAND
- http://taxes.marylandtaxes.com/Business_Taxes/Business_Tax_Types/Sales_and_Use_Tax/Tax_Information/Special_Situations/Purchases_for_Resale/

MASSACHUSETTS
- http://www.mass.gov/dor/forms/trustee/sales-and-use-tax/

MICHIGAN
- http://www.michigan.gov/uia/0,1607,7-118--89978--,00.html
- http://www.michigan.gov/taxes/0,1607,7-238-43529-155458--,00.html
- http://www.michigan.gov/taxes/0,1607,7-238-43519_43521-155365--,00.html

MINNESOTA
- http://www.revenue.state.mn.us/businesses/sut/Pages/File-and-Pay.aspx
- https://www.mndor.state.mn.us/tp/eservices/_/

MISSISSIPPI
- http://www.dor.ms.gov/taxareas/sales/reg.html

MISSOURI
- http://dor.mo.gov/business/sales/

MONTANA
- http://revenue.mt.gov/home/businesses/sales_tax.aspx

NEBRASKA
- http://www.revenue.ne.gov/salestax.html

NEVADA
- http://tax.nv.gov/Forms/General_Purpose_Forms/

NEW HAMPSHIRE
- http://www.revenue.nh.gov/assistance/resale-exempt-certs.htm
- http://www.sos.nh.gov/corporate/faqs.html#13

NEW JERSEY
- http://www.state.nj.us/treasury/taxation/prntsale.shtml
- http://www.state.nj.us/treasury/taxation/pdf/other_forms/sales/st3.pdf

NEW MEXICO
- http://www.tax.newmexico.gov/Businesses/non-taxable-transaction-certificates.aspx

NEW YORK
- http://www.tax.ny.gov/bus/st/stidx.htm

NORTH CAROLINA
- http://www.dor.state.nc.us/taxes/sales/

NORTH DAKOTA
- http://www.nd.gov/tax/salesanduse/forms/

OHIO
- http://www.tax.ohio.gov/Forms.aspx
- http://www.tax.ohio.gov/sales_and_use/registration.aspx

OKLAHOMA
- http://www.tax.ok.gov/howdoi13.html

OREGON

- http://www.oregon.gov/DOR/salestax.shtml

PENNSYLVANIA

- http://www.portal.state.pa.us/portal/server.pt/community/sales___use_tax/14702

RHODE ISLAND

- http://www.tax.ri.gov/taxforms/sales_excise/sales_use.php

SOUTH CAROLINA

- http://www.sctax.org/Tax+Information/Sales+and+Use+Tax/saleinfo.htm
- http://www.sctax.org/NR/rdonlyres/A66254B4-E02D-4D81-8327-1DC5187F2D42/0/ST8A.pdf

SOUTH DAKOTA

- https://www.sateng.com/resale/sd.pdf
- https://apps.sd.gov/RV23EPath/Login.aspx

TENNESSEE

- http://www.tn.gov/revenue/onlinefiling/salesanduse/salestaxefile.shtml

TEXAS

- http://www.cpa.state.tx.us/taxpermit/

UTAH

- http://tax.utah.gov/sales/

VERMONT
- http://www.state.vt.us/tax/formstrust.shtml

VIRGINIA
- http://www.tax.virginia.gov/site.cfm?alias=SalesUseTax#RetailSales
- http://www.tax.virginia.gov/ireg/

WASHINGTON
- https://fortress.wa.gov/dor/efile/MyAccount/ResellersPermit/Default.aspx
- https://fortress.wa.gov/dor/efile/FortressLogon/Logon.aspx

WEST VIRGINIA
- https://www.business4wv.com/b4wvpublic/default.aspx

WISCONSIN
- http://www.revenue.wi.gov/forms/sales/btr-101.pdf
- https://tap.revenue.wi.gov/services/_/

WYOMING
- http://revenue.wyo.gov/Excise-Tax-Division
- https://excise-wyifs.wy.gov/

TOOLS, SUPPLIES AND SUPPLIERS WE USE

While online selling doesn't require a lot in the way of tools and equipment, it does require some. We've gathered together this list of tools, supplies and suppliers we use in our online businesses. There is some duplication, because Darla may use one service while Charlene uses another.

Be sure to visit our Resource page at

http://wholesalesourcingexperts.com/resources/

for links and more information about the tools, supplies and suppliers we use.

SOFTWARE, SERVICES AND SUPPLIERS

- Appeagle
- Auctiva
- Bubblefast

- Endicia
- Excel or Google Docs
- Feedback Five
- GoDaddy
- Inkfrog.com
- Inventory Lab
- List Label Ship
- Quickbooks
- Repriceit
- Sellbrite
- TaxJar
- Uline
- UPS
- USPS

SUPPLIES AND EQUIPMENT

- Air pillows
- Black permanent markers
- Blow dryer or heat gun
- Boxes
- Box resizer tool
- Bubble wrap
- Dymo printer
- File folders
- House Labels brand labels
- Impulse sealer
- Laser printer
- Newsprint end rolls and other void fill
- Poly bags
- Prepping table

- Round seals, clear
- Scale
- Scotty Peelers
- Shelving
- Shipping tape
- Shrink wrap
- Shipping labels
- "Single Item Enclosed" labels
- Stretch wrap on a stick
- Sticky notes
- Storage for bags, shrink wrap and bubble wrap
- Suffocation warning labels
- "This is a Set, Do Not Separate" labels

LIMITS OF LIABILITY AND DISCLAIMER OF WARRANTY

NOTICE: You do not have the right to reprint or resell this book. You may not give away, sell, or share the content contained herein.

If you purchased an electronic version of this book, feel free to print out a copy for your personal use. We like to have a hard copy of reference books such as this so that we can hold it in our hands, read, and mark up with notes and checklists.

The authors and publisher of this book have used their best efforts in preparing this book. The authors and publisher make no representation or warranties with respect to the accuracy, applicability, fitness, or completeness of the contents of this program. They disclaim any warranties (expressed or implied), merchantability, or fitness for any particular purpose. The authors and the publisher shall in no event be held liable for any loss or other damages, including but not limited to special, incidental, consequential, or other damages.

As always, the advice of a competent legal, tax, accounting or other professional should be sought.

The authors and publisher do not warrant the performance, effectiveness, or applicability of any sites listed in this book. All links are for information purposes only and are not warranted for content, accuracy or any other implied or explicit purpose.

The material in this book does not constitute legal advice, only the author's interpretation of the laws involved as they understand them. As always, when embarking on any business venture, legal advice should be obtained from a competent legal professional.

This book contains material protected under International and Federal Copyright Laws and Treaties. Any unauthorized reprint or use of this material is prohibited.

Some links in this book are affiliate links. This means that if you click on the link and make a purchase, we will make a commission from the sale of the product. We are disclosing this in accordance with the Federal Trade Commission's 16 CFR, Part 255: "Guides Concerning the Use of Endorsements and Testimonials in Advertising." Please feel free to go directly to the websites if you wish to avoid the authors receiving any affiliate income for introducing you to the product.

The authors of this book in no way represent or are employed by any of the companies mentioned in this book.

ABOUT THE AUTHORS

 **Charlene Anderson** is an experienced and respected eCommerce seller and jewelry and textile artist. She started selling on eBay in 1998 and on Amazon in 2002, and has grown her business from a $100 investment to a business that grosses in the mid-six figures ... all without employees! Known for her organizational skills, business smarts and enthusiasm, Charlene brings a lifetime of entrepreneurial experience to the table.

 **Darla Flack** has been leading her family run eCommerce business since 2007, selling into the high-six figures. Darla believes success is not well won without bringing others along on the journey. Darla enjoys coaching others using her unique mixture of encouragement, straight talk, strong guidance and humor.

16368646R00086

Made in the USA
Middletown, DE
12 December 2014